© 2024 by FAISAL JAMIL. All rights reserved.

Title: "Empower: The Global Journey of Women's Rights"

This book, along with its contents encompassing text, illustrations, images, diagrams, and other creative elements, is the exclusive property of FAISAL JAMIL and is safeguarded by copyright law.

FAISAL JAMIL asserts full ownership and retains all rights to this book. No part of this publication may be reproduced, distributed, or transmitted in any form or by any means, such as photocopying, recording, or electronic methods, without prior written consent from the copyright holder. Brief quotations in critical reviews and certain noncommercial uses permitted by copyright law are exceptions.

This copyright notice applies to all editions, formats, and translations of the book, whether in print, digital, or any other medium or technology existing now or developed in the future. Unauthorized use or infringement may result in legal action and pursuit of remedies under applicable copyright laws.

While efforts have been made to ensure accuracy and reliability, FAISAL JAMIL does not guarantee the completeness or suitability of the information. Readers are responsible for evaluating and using the content judiciously.

FAISAL JAMIL reserves the right to make changes, updates, or corrections to the book without prior notice. Inclusion of third-party materials or references does not imply endorsement or affiliation unless used under fair use principles or with proper permissions and attributions.

For permissions, inquiries, or requests regarding the book's use, please contact FAISAL JAMIL through official channels listed on their Amazon author page or provided email address.

This comprehensive copyright notice serves to protect FAISAL JAMIL'S intellectual property rights, maintain content control, and inform users about associated restrictions and permissions.

Warm regards,

FAISAL JAMIL

I Always Give's Free Copies Need Your Feedback And

Reviews Keeps In Touch!

http://www.amazon.com/author/faisal.jamil

Email: faisaljamilauthor@gmail.com

About the author

Certainly! Faisal Jamil is a multifaceted individual with a diverse set of skills and experiences. With a strong foundation in computer knowledge since childhood, he has developed a deep understanding of technology that informs his work as a content writer. Faisal also possesses digital skills, which further enhance his abilities in various digital platforms and technologies.

Beyond his professional endeavors, Faisal Jamil has also excelled in the martial arts, particularly Shotokan Karate, where he achieved the prestigious rank of first Dan black belt. This achievement speaks to his dedication, discipline, and commitment to personal growth and mastery.

In his professional life, Faisal Jamil has carved out a successful career in sales management within the Fast Moving Consumer Goods (FMCG) sector. His roles in various FMCG companies have honed his skills in strategic planning, team leadership, and business development. Faisal's ability to drive sales and achieve targets has been instrumental in his career progression, showcasing his talent for identifying opportunities and delivering results.

Faisal Jamil is also deeply interested in business investment strategies, planning, and execution. His understanding of these areas has been key to his success in the business world, allowing him to make informed decisions and implement effective strategies. His ability to navigate the complexities of investment planning and execution has set him apart as a strategic thinker and a valuable asset in any business endeavor.

Overall, Faisal Jamil is a dynamic individual who combines his passion for technology, martial arts, sales management, digital skills, and business investment strategies to achieve success in diverse fields. His journey is a testament to his versatility, resilience, and continuous pursuit of excellence.

Yours Sincerely

FAISAL JAMIL

I Always Give's Free Copies Need Your Feedback And Reviews Keeps In Touch!

https://www.amazon.com/author/faisal.jamil

Email: faisaljamilauthor@gmail.com

EMPOWER
THE GLOBAL JOURNEY OF
WOMEN'S RIGHTS

Table of Content

Introduction

Chapter 1: The Dawn of Women's Rights

Chapter 2: The Suffrage Movement

Chapter 3: The Rise of Feminism in the 20th Century

Chapter 4: Women in the Workforce

Chapter 5: Education and Empowerment

Chapter 6: Women's Health and Reproductive Rights

Chapter 7: Violence Against Women

Chapter 8: Women in Politics

Chapter 9: Intersectionality in the Women's Rights Movement

Chapter 10: The Role of Men in Advancing Women's Rights

Chapter 11: Women and the Media

Chapter 12: Women in Science and Technology

Chapter 13: Economic Empowerment and Microfinance

Chapter 14: Global Perspectives on Women's Rights

Chapter 15: Women and Environmental Activism

Chapter 16: Legal Milestones in Women's Rights

Chapter 17: The Role of NGOs and Grassroots Movements

Chapter 18: The Future of Women's Rights

Chapter 19: Personal Stories of Empowerment

Chapter 20: A Call to Action

Epilogue: Reflecting on Progress and Paving the Way Forward

INTRODUCTION

"Empower: The Global Journey of Women's Rights" invites readers on a transformative journey through the history and ongoing struggle for gender equality. This book explores the myriad ways women have fought for their rights, highlighting their resilience, courage, and unyielding determination to achieve equality.

The Significance of Women's Rights

The fight for women's rights is not merely a struggle for half of the population but a fundamental quest for justice, human dignity, and societal progress. When women are empowered and granted equal opportunities, entire communities and nations benefit. Gender equality fosters economic growth, enhances political stability, and nurtures healthier, more educated societies. Yet, despite significant progress, women worldwide continue to face systemic discrimination, violence, and unequal opportunities.

Historical Roots and Pioneering Voices

Our journey begins with the foundational efforts of early feminists and suffragists who dared to challenge the status quo. Figures such as Mary Wollstonecraft, who advocated for women's education in the 18th century, Elizabeth Cady Stanton, who fought tirelessly for women's suffrage in the United States, and Sojourner Truth, whose powerful speeches demanded intersectional equality, laid the groundwork for future generations. These pioneers ignited a movement that has evolved and expanded over centuries.

Global Struggle and Milestones

The book delves into the global fight for women's suffrage, examining key milestones in various countries and the profound impact of women securing the right to vote. From the passionate protests in the United Kingdom to the tireless activism in New Zealand, each story underscores the global nature of this struggle. These victories were not just political but deeply personal, empowering women to seek further equality in all aspects of life.

The Evolution of Feminism

The narrative then explores the evolution of feminism through the 20th century, marked by the second-wave movement. This era brought a broader focus on issues such as reproductive rights, workplace equality, and sexual liberation. Influential texts like Betty Friedan's "The Feminine Mystique" and the activism of leaders like Gloria Steinem spurred a cultural shift towards gender equality, influencing legislation and societal attitudes.

Contemporary Challenges and Achievements

As we move into contemporary times, the book examines the diverse challenges and achievements women face today. From breaking barriers in the workforce and leadership roles to confronting violence and advocating for reproductive rights, women continue to push boundaries and redefine their roles in society. The concept of intersectionality is introduced, emphasizing the importance of an inclusive movement that addresses the unique experiences of marginalized women.

A Call to Action

The book concludes with a call to action, urging readers to participate in the ongoing struggle for gender equality. It highlights practical steps individuals, organizations, and governments can take to support women's rights and foster an equitable world. Reflecting on past achievements and recognizing the challenges ahead, "Empower" serves as both a chronicle of progress and a roadmap for the future.

Why This Book Matters

"Empower: The Global Journey of Women's Rights" is not just a historical account but a celebration of the indomitable spirit of women who have fought, and continue to fight, for equality. It aims to inspire readers to join this vital movement, understanding that the fight for women's rights is integral to the broader quest for human rights and justice. By learning from the past and committing to the future, we can collectively ensure that gender equality is not just an aspiration but a reality for all.

Welcome to a journey of empowerment, resilience, and transformation.

Chapter 1
The Dawn of Women's Rights

Introduction

The struggle for women's rights is a long and complex journey, marked by numerous pivotal moments and influential figures. The dawn of the women's rights movement can be traced back to the late 18th and early 19th centuries, a period of social upheaval and intellectual awakening. This chapter explores the origins of this transformative movement, focusing on early feminists and suffragists who laid the groundwork for future advocacy.

The Early Feminists

Mary Wollstonecraft

Mary Wollstonecraft is often regarded as one of the founding figures of the women's rights movement. Born in 1759 in England, Wollstonecraft's seminal work, "A Vindication of the Rights of Woman" (1792), is a cornerstone of feminist literature. In this groundbreaking text, Wollstonecraft argued that women were not naturally inferior to men but appeared so because they lacked education. She advocated for equal educational opportunities for women, asserting that women could contribute significantly to society if given the same educational opportunities as men.

Wollstonecraft's ideas were revolutionary for her time. She challenged the traditional roles of women and questioned the societal norms that confined women to domestic spheres. Her work inspired future generations of feminists and established a theoretical framework for the movement.

Elizabeth Cady Stanton

Elizabeth Cady Stanton was a central figure in the early American women's rights movement. Born in 1815, Stanton was a social activist, abolitionist, and leading figure of the early women's rights movement. She is best known for her role in organizing the Seneca Falls Convention in 1848, the first women's rights convention in the United States.

The Seneca Falls Convention marked a significant turning point in the women's rights movement. At this convention, Stanton presented the Declaration of Sentiments, a document modeled after the Declaration of Independence, which outlined the grievances and demands of women. The Declaration called for equal rights for women, including the right to vote, which was a radical demand at the time.

Stanton's work extended beyond the Seneca Falls Convention. She collaborated with other prominent activists, including Susan B. Anthony, to push for women's suffrage and other social reforms. Stanton's advocacy and writings helped shape the direction of the women's rights movement in the United States.

The Role of Abolitionism

The abolitionist movement, which sought to end slavery in the United States, played a significant role in the development of the women's rights movement. Many early women's rights activists, including Stanton and Lucretia

Mott, were deeply involved in the abolitionist cause. The struggle for the rights of enslaved people highlighted the broader issues of human rights and social justice, inspiring women to fight for their own rights.

Sojourner Truth

Sojourner Truth, born into slavery as Isabella Baumfree in 1797, was a powerful advocate for both abolition and women's rights. After gaining her freedom in 1826, Truth became a prominent speaker and activist. Her famous speech, "Ain't I a Woman?", delivered at the Ohio Women's Rights Convention in 1851, remains one of the most eloquent and poignant expressions of the intersection of race and gender in the fight for equality.

In her speech, Truth challenged prevailing notions of racial and gender inferiority. She pointed out the physical and intellectual capabilities of women, particularly Black women, arguing that they deserved the same rights and opportunities as men. Truth's activism highlighted the interconnectedness of the struggles for racial and gender equality and emphasized the need for an inclusive approach to human rights.

Building the Foundation

The early efforts of feminists and suffragists laid a critical foundation for the women's rights movement. These pioneers faced significant opposition and societal resistance, yet their determination and resilience set the stage for future progress.

Education and Advocacy

Education played a pivotal role in the early women's rights movement. Figures like Wollstonecraft advocated for women's education as a means to achieve equality. Educational opportunities for women slowly began to expand in the 19th century, leading to the establishment of women's colleges and increased access to higher education.

In addition to education, advocacy and public speaking were crucial in raising awareness and garnering support for women's rights. Activists like Stanton and Truth used their voices to challenge societal norms and inspire others to join the cause.

The International Context

While much of the early women's rights movement is often centered on Western figures and events, it is important to recognize the global dimensions of the struggle. Women around the world were also fighting for their rights, often in different cultural and political contexts.

Early International Movements

In Europe, the women's rights movement gained momentum with figures like Emmeline Pankhurst in the United Kingdom, who founded the Women's Social and Political Union (WSPU) in 1903. The WSPU adopted militant tactics to demand voting rights for women, significantly influencing the suffrage movement in Britain.

In other parts of the world, women were organizing and advocating for their rights as well. For example, in India, figures like Savitribai Phule and Tarabai Shinde challenged caste and gender discrimination in the 19th century, emphasizing the need for educational and social reforms.

Conclusion

The dawn of the women's rights movement was marked by the efforts of pioneering feminists and suffragists who challenged the status quo and fought for equality. Mary Wollstonecraft, Elizabeth Cady Stanton, Sojourner Truth, and many others laid the groundwork for future advocacy by highlighting the importance of education, public speaking, and inclusive approaches to human rights. Their legacy continues to inspire and guide the ongoing struggle for women's rights around the world.

As we move forward in this book, we will explore how these early efforts evolved and how the women's rights movement has impacted societies globally. The journey that began with these trailblazers set in motion a transformative movement that continues to shape the world today.

Chapter 2
The Suffrage Movement

Introduction

The fight for women's suffrage was a pivotal chapter in the broader struggle for gender equality. Securing the right to vote was not only a matter of political inclusion but also a powerful symbol of women's autonomy and citizenship. This chapter delves into the global suffrage movement, highlighting significant milestones in the United States, the United Kingdom, and other countries. We will explore how this hard-won right empowered women to pursue further equality and transformed societies worldwide.

The Suffrage Movement in the United States

Early Beginnings

The suffrage movement in the United States can be traced back to the mid-19th century, with the 1848 Seneca Falls Convention marking a significant starting point. Organized by Elizabeth Cady Stanton and Lucretia Mott, this convention was the first of its kind dedicated to discussing women's rights. The Declaration of Sentiments, presented by Stanton, called for equal rights for women, including the right to vote.

Key Figures and Organizations

Susan B. Anthony:

A close collaborator with Stanton, Anthony was a leading figure in the American suffrage movement. She co-founded the National Woman Suffrage Association (NWSA) in 1869, which focused on securing a federal amendment for women's suffrage.

Alice Paul:

A more radical suffragist, Paul founded the National Woman's Party (NWP) in 1916. She organized parades, protests, and hunger strikes to draw attention to the cause. Paul's efforts were instrumental in the passage of the 19th Amendment.

Ida B. Wells:

An African American journalist and activist, Wells highlighted the intersection of race and gender in the suffrage movement. She founded the Alpha Suffrage Club in Chicago to address the needs of Black women.

The 19th Amendment

After decades of tireless campaigning, the 19th Amendment to the U.S. Constitution was ratified on August 18, 1920. This amendment prohibited the states and the federal government from denying the right to vote to citizens on the basis of sex. The passage of the 19th Amendment marked a monumental victory for the suffrage movement and significantly expanded the electorate, empowering millions of women to participate in the democratic process.

The Suffrage Movement in the United Kingdom

Early Activism

The fight for women's suffrage in the United Kingdom began in earnest in the mid-19th century, with the formation of various suffrage societies. The first petition for women's suffrage was presented to Parliament in 1866 by John Stuart Mill, a philosopher and Member of Parliament, and supported by suffragists like Lydia Becker.

The Suffragettes and the Suffragists

Millicent Fawcett:

Leader of the National Union of Women's Suffrage Societies (NUWSS), Fawcett and her followers, known as suffragists, employed peaceful and lawful methods to advocate for women's suffrage.

Emmeline Pankhurst:

In contrast, Pankhurst founded the Women's Social and Political Union (WSPU) in 1903. The WSPU, known for its militant tactics, aimed to draw public attention through acts of civil disobedience, such as hunger strikes, window smashing, and public demonstrations.

The Representation of the People Act 1918

World War I significantly influenced the suffrage movement in the UK. Women's substantial contributions to the war effort helped shift public opinion in favor of granting them the vote. The Representation of the People Act 1918 enfranchised women over the age of 30 who met minimum property qualifications. It wasn't until the Equal Franchise Act of 1928 that women gained voting rights on par with men, allowing all women over the age of 21 to vote.

Global Suffrage Movements

New Zealand: The Pioneer

New Zealand was the first country in the world to grant women the right to vote in parliamentary elections. The Electoral Act of 1893 was a result of extensive campaigning by suffragists like Kate Sheppard. This landmark achievement set a precedent for other countries and inspired suffrage movements worldwide.

Australia

Australia followed New Zealand's example, granting women the right to vote and stand for election at the federal level in 1902. However, it wasn't until much later that Indigenous Australian women gained full voting rights, highlighting the intersection of race and gender in the suffrage struggle.

Scandinavia

The Nordic countries were early adopters of women's suffrage. Finland granted women the right to vote in 1906, followed by Norway in 1913, Denmark and Iceland in 1915, and Sweden in 1921. These countries also allowed women to stand for parliamentary elections, leading to significant female representation in government.

Other Notable Examples

Russia:

After the Russian Revolution, women gained the right to vote in 1917, reflecting the broader social changes brought about by the revolution.

Germany:

Women's suffrage was introduced in 1918 following the end of World War I and the establishment of the Weimar Republic.

Turkey:

Under the leadership of Mustafa Kemal Atatürk, Turkish women gained the right to vote in municipal elections in 1930 and in national elections in 1934.

The Impact of Women's Suffrage

Political Empowerment

Securing the right to vote allowed women to influence political decisions and policies directly. Women began to run for office, hold public positions, and shape legislative agendas. This political empowerment was crucial in addressing issues such as labor rights, education, healthcare, and social welfare.

Social and Cultural Transformation

The suffrage movement also catalyzed broader social and cultural changes. It challenged traditional gender roles and paved the way for women to participate more fully in public life. Women's increased visibility and participation in politics inspired subsequent generations to continue advocating for gender equality in all areas of society.

Economic Impact

The right to vote enabled women to advocate for economic policies that addressed their needs and interests. Issues such as equal pay, labor rights, and economic independence became central to the feminist agenda. As women gained political power, they could push for legislation that supported their economic empowerment.

Conclusion

The global fight for women's suffrage was a monumental struggle that spanned decades and continents. The efforts of countless women and their allies to secure the right to vote fundamentally transformed societies and laid the groundwork for continued advancements in gender equality. The suffrage movement demonstrated the power of collective action and set a precedent for future generations to pursue justice and equality.

As we move forward in this book, we will explore how the right to vote, once secured, empowered women to seek further equality and address a wide range of issues affecting their lives. The suffrage movement was not the end but rather the beginning of an ongoing journey towards full equality and empowerment for women around the world.

Chapter 3
The Rise of Feminism in the 20th Century

Introduction

The 20th century witnessed significant developments in the feminist movement, marked by the emergence of the second-wave feminism that broadened the scope of issues beyond suffrage to include a wide array of social, political, and economic concerns. This chapter explores the evolution of feminism through the 20th century, focusing on key events, influential publications, and the impact of prominent feminist leaders.

The Early 20th Century: Beyond Suffrage

Post-Suffrage Era

After achieving the right to vote, women in many countries began to turn their attention to other issues of inequality. The early 20th century saw women advocating for equal rights in education, employment, and reproductive health. Organizations such as the League of Women Voters in the United States emerged to continue the fight for women's rights and promote civic engagement.

World War II and Women's Roles

World War II had a profound impact on women's roles in society. As men went to war, women filled the labor shortages by working in factories, offices, and other traditionally male-dominated jobs. This shift challenged traditional gender roles and demonstrated women's capabilities in various fields. However, post-war societal norms often pressured women to return to domestic roles, setting the stage for future feminist movements.

The Second Wave of Feminism

The second-wave feminism, beginning in the early 1960s, was characterized by a renewed and more radical push for gender equality. This wave focused on a broader range of issues, including sexuality, family, workplace rights, and reproductive freedom.

The Feminine Mystique

One of the pivotal moments that sparked the second-wave feminist movement was the publication of Betty Friedan's "The Feminine Mystique" in 1963. Friedan's book critiqued the idealized image of suburban housewives and the notion that women could find fulfillment solely through homemaking and motherhood. She identified "the problem that has no name," describing the dissatisfaction and sense of unfulfillment experienced by many women.

"The Feminine Mystique" resonated with a large number of women, bringing attention to the widespread discontent and igniting a collective consciousness about gender inequality. Friedan's work is often credited with catalyzing the second-wave feminist movement.

Formation of NOW

In 1966, Betty Friedan, along with other activists, founded the National Organization for Women (NOW). NOW aimed to address a wide range of issues affecting women, including workplace discrimination, reproductive rights, and political representation. The organization adopted a more militant stance compared to earlier women's groups, pushing for immediate legal and societal changes.

NOW's founding statement called for "true equality for all women in America" and emphasized the need to eliminate discrimination and promote equal opportunities in all aspects of life. The organization played a crucial role in lobbying for legislative changes, raising public awareness, and supporting women's rights.

Key Events and Legislative Milestones

Equal Pay Act of 1963

The Equal Pay Act, passed in 1963, was a significant legislative achievement of the second-wave feminist movement. It aimed to abolish wage disparity based on gender, making it illegal for employers to pay women less than men for the same work. Although enforcement was initially weak, the act set an important legal precedent for gender equality in the workplace.

Title IX

Title IX of the Education Amendments Act of 1972 was another landmark victory for the feminist movement. This federal law prohibited sex-based discrimination in any education program or activity receiving federal financial assistance. Title IX had a profound impact on increasing opportunities for women in education and athletics, leading to greater gender parity in these fields.

Roe v. Wade

In 1973, the U.S. Supreme Court's decision in Roe v. Wade was a monumental victory for reproductive rights. The ruling recognized a woman's constitutional right to privacy, effectively legalizing abortion nationwide. This decision was a major triumph for feminist activists who had long campaigned for women's reproductive freedom and control over their own bodies.

Prominent Feminist Leaders

Gloria Steinem

Gloria Steinem emerged as one of the most influential figures of the second-wave feminist movement. A journalist and social activist, Steinem co-founded Ms. magazine in 1971, providing a platform for feminist voices and issues. Her articulate advocacy and charismatic presence made her a prominent spokesperson for the movement.

Steinem's work extended beyond writing and journalism. She co-founded several organizations, including the Women's Action Alliance and the National Women's Political Caucus, which aimed to increase women's participation in politics and advocate for policy changes. Steinem's influence helped shape public discourse on feminism and gender equality.

Shirley Chisholm

Shirley Chisholm was a trailblazer in American politics. In 1968, she became the first African American woman elected to the U.S. Congress. Chisholm was a fierce advocate for women's rights, civil rights, and social justice.

In 1972, she made history again by becoming the first African American woman to run for the Democratic Party's presidential nomination. Chisholm's political career and advocacy highlighted the intersectionality of race and gender in the fight for equality.

Betty Friedan

Beyond her role in writing "The Feminine Mystique," Betty Friedan continued to be a driving force in the feminist movement. As a co-founder of NOW, she worked tirelessly to address gender discrimination and promote women's rights. Friedan also played a significant role in organizing the Women's Strike for Equality in 1970, which marked the 50th anniversary of the 19th Amendment and drew attention to ongoing gender inequalities.

Broader Impacts and Global Reach

International Women's Year and the UN Decade for Women

The feminist movement in the United States and other Western countries had a global influence. In 1975, the United Nations declared International Women's Year and held the first World Conference on Women in Mexico City. This event marked the beginning of the UN Decade for Women (1976-1985), which aimed to promote gender equality and women's empowerment worldwide.

Feminist Movements Around the World

Feminist movements in other parts of the world were also gaining momentum. In Latin America, Asia, Africa, and Europe, women were organizing and advocating for their rights. For example, in India, the women's movement addressed issues such as dowry violence, workplace harassment, and political representation. In Africa, feminist leaders like Funmilayo Ransome-Kuti in Nigeria and Wangari Maathai in Kenya fought for women's rights and environmental justice.

Challenges and Criticisms

Intersectionality and Inclusivity

While the second-wave feminist movement made significant strides, it faced criticisms for its lack of inclusivity and attention to the intersectionality of race, class, and sexuality. Many women of color, working-class women, and LGBTQ+ individuals felt marginalized within the mainstream feminist movement.

In response to these criticisms, the concept of intersectionality, coined by Kimberlé Crenshaw in the late 1980s, gained prominence. Intersectionality emphasized the interconnectedness of various forms of oppression and the need for a more inclusive feminist agenda that addressed the diverse experiences of all women.

Conclusion

The rise of feminism in the 20th century, particularly the second-wave movement, marked a period of profound social, political, and cultural transformation. Key events, influential publications, and the tireless efforts of feminist leaders brought attention to a wide range of issues affecting women and pushed for significant legislative changes.

As we continue this journey through the history of women's rights, we will see how the foundations laid by the second-wave feminist movement paved the way for further advancements and challenges in the ongoing fight for gender equality. The legacy of the 20th-century feminism continues to inspire and inform contemporary feminist movements around the world, highlighting the enduring importance of advocacy, solidarity, and intersectionality in the pursuit of justice and equality for all women.

Chapter 4
Women in the Workforce

Introduction

The participation of women in the workforce has been a dynamic and transformative aspect of modern history. From facing severe discrimination and limited opportunities to making significant strides in various fields, women have continuously challenged and reshaped workplace norms. This chapter delves into the historical barriers women have faced, such as gender discrimination and pay inequality, and highlights the progress made through key legislation like the Equal Pay Act. We will also explore the increasing presence of women in leadership roles and the ongoing challenges they encounter.

Historical Barriers

Early 20th Century Workforce

At the beginning of the 20th century, women's roles in the workforce were largely confined to a few select industries, such as textiles, teaching, and domestic service. Society's expectation was for women to prioritize home and family over career aspirations. Women who worked outside the home often faced harsh working conditions, low pay, and limited opportunities for advancement.

Gender Discrimination

Gender discrimination in the workplace has been a persistent issue throughout history. Women were frequently denied jobs based on their gender or were paid less than their male counterparts for the same work. Discriminatory practices included:

Hiring and Promotion:

Women were often passed over for jobs and promotions in favor of men, regardless of qualifications or experience.

Occupational Segregation:

Certain jobs were deemed "appropriate" for women, leading to occupational segregation that confined women to lower-paying, less prestigious positions.

Workplace Harassment:

Women faced sexual harassment and hostile work environments, which further hindered their professional progress.

Legislative Progress

Equal Pay Act of 1963

The Equal Pay Act of 1963 was a landmark piece of legislation in the United States aimed at addressing wage disparity based on gender. The Act mandated that men and women receive equal pay for equal work performed under similar working conditions. Despite its passage, enforcement was initially weak, and wage gaps persisted, necessitating further advocacy and legal action.

Title VII of the Civil Rights Act of 1964

Title VII of the Civil Rights Act of 1964 made it illegal for employers to discriminate against employees based on race, color, religion, sex, or national origin. This legislation provided a legal framework for women to challenge discriminatory practices in the workplace and seek justice through the courts. It also established the Equal Employment Opportunity Commission (EEOC) to enforce anti-discrimination laws.

Family and Medical Leave Act of 1993

The Family and Medical Leave Act (FMLA) of 1993 provided job-protected, unpaid leave for employees to deal with family and medical issues, including childbirth and caregiving responsibilities. This legislation was crucial in supporting working women, particularly mothers, by allowing them to take necessary leave without fear of losing their jobs.

Progress and Achievements

Increased Workforce Participation

Over the past century, women's participation in the workforce has significantly increased. According to the U.S. Bureau of Labor Statistics, the labor force participation rate for women rose from approximately 33% in 1950 to nearly 60% by the end of the 20th century. This increase reflects changing societal norms, greater educational opportunities, and evolving economic demands.

Education and Professional Advancement

Access to higher education has been a critical factor in advancing women's careers. As more women attained college degrees and professional qualifications, they were able to pursue careers in previously male-dominated fields such as law, medicine, engineering, and business.

Women in Leadership

The presence of women in leadership roles has grown steadily, though disparities remain. Women have increasingly occupied positions of power and influence in various sectors:

Politics:

Women have made significant strides in political leadership. For example, Margaret Thatcher became the first female Prime Minister of the United Kingdom in 1979, and Angela Merkel served as Chancellor of Germany from 2005 to 2021. In the United States, Kamala Harris was elected as the first female Vice President in 2020.

Corporate Leadership:

The number of women in executive positions and on corporate boards has also increased. Women like Mary Barra, CEO of General Motors, and Ginni Rometty, former CEO of IBM, have broken barriers in the corporate world.

Academia and STEM:

Women have made notable contributions in academia and STEM (Science, Technology, Engineering, and Mathematics) fields. Prominent figures include Nobel laureate Malala Yousafzai, a Pakistani activist for girls' education, and astrophysicist Jocelyn Bell Burnell, who co-discovered the first radio pulsars.

Ongoing Challenges

Despite significant progress, women continue to face numerous challenges in the workforce.

Gender Pay Gap

The gender pay gap remains a pervasive issue. On average, women still earn less than men for comparable work. Factors contributing to the pay gap include occupational segregation, differences in work experience, and discrimination. Efforts to close the gap include advocating for transparency in pay practices and promoting policies that support pay equity.

Work-Life Balance

Balancing work and family responsibilities is a significant challenge for many women. Societal expectations and inadequate support systems, such as affordable childcare and parental leave, place additional burdens on working mothers. Employers and policymakers are increasingly recognizing the need for family-friendly workplace policies to support work-life balance.

Glass Ceiling

The "glass ceiling" refers to the invisible barriers that prevent women from advancing to the highest levels of leadership and decision-making positions. While women have made strides in many areas, they are still underrepresented in top executive roles and board positions. Initiatives to address this include mentorship programs, diversity and inclusion efforts, and policies aimed at promoting women's advancement.

Sexual Harassment and Workplace Culture

Sexual harassment and hostile work environments continue to be significant issues for women. The #MeToo movement, which gained momentum in 2017, brought global attention to the prevalence of sexual harassment and assault in the workplace. Efforts to combat this include stricter policies, better reporting mechanisms, and cultural shifts toward zero tolerance for harassment.

Case Studies of Success

Iceland's Gender Equality Model

Iceland is often cited as a model for gender equality. The country has consistently ranked high on the World Economic Forum's Global Gender Gap Index. Iceland has implemented progressive policies, such as mandatory parental leave for both mothers and fathers, and a requirement for companies to prove they are paying men and women equally.

Rwanda's Political Leadership

Rwanda has achieved remarkable gender parity in political representation. Following the 1994 genocide, women played a crucial role in rebuilding the nation. Today, women hold more than 60% of seats in the Rwandan parliament, the highest percentage of any country in the world. This representation has led to significant legislative and social advancements for women in Rwanda.

Conclusion

The journey of women in the workforce is one of resilience, progress, and ongoing challenges. From early struggles against gender discrimination and limited opportunities to significant legislative victories and the breaking of glass ceilings, women have made remarkable strides in reshaping the workplace. The continued efforts to address pay inequality, work-life balance, and workplace harassment are crucial in ensuring that the progress made so far is sustained and built upon.

As we continue to explore the history and impact of women's rights, it is essential to recognize the contributions of women in the workforce and the need for ongoing advocacy and policy reforms. The successes and challenges of women in the workplace serve as a testament to the transformative power of gender equality and the importance of creating inclusive and supportive environments for all.

Chapter 5
Education and Empowerment

Introduction

Education is a fundamental human right and a powerful tool for advancing women's rights and gender equality. It plays a crucial role in empowering women, enabling them to participate fully in society, and improving their economic, social, and political status. This chapter analyzes the role of education in advancing women's rights, explores global disparities in access to education for girls and women, and examines the transformative impact education has on their lives and communities.

The Role of Education in Advancing Women's Rights

Empowerment Through Knowledge

Education equips women with the knowledge and skills necessary to make informed decisions about their lives. It fosters critical thinking, enhances self-esteem, and provides women with the tools to challenge societal norms and advocate for their rights. Educated women are more likely to participate in the workforce, engage in political processes, and contribute to the economic development of their communities.

Economic Empowerment

Education is closely linked to economic empowerment. Women with higher levels of education tend to have better job opportunities, higher incomes, and greater financial independence. Educated women are more likely to start their own businesses, access credit, and invest in their families and communities. This economic empowerment reduces poverty and contributes to overall economic growth.

Social and Health Benefits

Educated women tend to have better health outcomes for themselves and their families. They are more likely to seek healthcare services, practice healthy behaviors, and make informed decisions about reproductive health. Education also reduces child mortality rates, as educated mothers are more likely to ensure their children receive proper nutrition and medical care.

Global Disparities in Access to Education

Despite the recognized importance of education, significant disparities exist in access to education for girls and women worldwide. These disparities are influenced by various factors, including socio-economic status, cultural norms, geographic location, and conflict.

Socio-Economic Barriers

Poverty is a major barrier to education for girls. In many low-income countries, families prioritize boys' education over girls' due to limited resources. Girls may be required to work, care for siblings, or marry early, preventing them from attending school. The cost of school fees, uniforms, and supplies also poses a significant obstacle.

Cultural and Social Norms

In some cultures, traditional gender roles and norms discourage girls from pursuing education. Societal expectations that prioritize marriage and childbearing over education for girls hinder their access to schooling. Additionally, issues such as gender-based violence, early marriage, and discriminatory practices further limit girls' educational opportunities.

Geographic and Infrastructure Challenges

Rural and remote areas often lack adequate educational infrastructure, including schools, qualified teachers, and learning materials. Long distances to schools, unsafe travel routes, and poor sanitation facilities disproportionately affect girls' ability to attend and complete school.

Conflict and Crisis

Conflict and crisis situations severely impact girls' education. Schools may be destroyed, and educational systems disrupted, leaving children without access to learning. Girls are particularly vulnerable in conflict zones, facing increased risks of violence, exploitation, and displacement, which hinder their educational opportunities.

Transformative Impact of Education

Individual Empowerment and Agency

Education empowers women by providing them with the knowledge and skills to make informed choices about their lives. Educated women are more likely to delay marriage and childbirth, seek employment, and participate in community and political activities. This individual empowerment translates into greater agency and decision-making power within their families and communities.

Economic Growth and Development

Educating girls and women has a profound impact on economic growth and development. Studies have shown that increasing the number of educated women in the workforce boosts productivity and economic output. Educated women are more likely to invest in their children's education, creating a positive cycle of intergenerational progress and economic stability.

Health and Well-Being

Education has a direct impact on health and well-being. Educated women are more likely to access healthcare services, adopt healthy behaviors, and make informed decisions about reproductive health. This leads to improved maternal and child health outcomes, reduced fertility rates, and lower infant and child mortality rates.

Social Change and Gender Equality

Education is a powerful driver of social change and gender equality. It challenges traditional gender norms and stereotypes, promotes women's rights, and fosters attitudes of respect and equality. Educated women are more likely to advocate for themselves and others, leading to greater gender parity in various aspects of life, including politics, business, and community leadership.

Case Studies and Success Stories

Malala Yousafzai and Girls' Education

Malala Yousafzai, a Pakistani activist, is a prominent advocate for girls' education. After surviving an assassination attempt by the Taliban for her activism, Malala continued to champion the right to education for girls worldwide. She co-authored the memoir "I Am Malala" and established the Malala Fund, which supports education initiatives for girls in conflict-affected areas. Malala's story highlights the transformative power of education and the importance of advocating for girls' rights.

Rwanda's Commitment to Education

Rwanda has made significant strides in promoting girls' education. Following the 1994 genocide, the country prioritized education as a means of rebuilding and fostering social cohesion. Rwanda implemented policies to ensure equal access to education, including free primary education and gender-sensitive curricula. As a result, the country achieved gender parity in primary and secondary school enrollment, with girls' educational attainment contributing to national development and social progress.

Educate Girls Program in India

The Educate Girls program in India focuses on improving access to education for girls in rural and underserved communities. The program mobilizes community volunteers, known as Team Balika, to identify out-of-school girls, enroll them in schools, and support their retention and academic performance. Educate Girls has successfully increased enrollment rates and reduced dropout rates, demonstrating the impact of community-driven initiatives in advancing girls' education.

Challenges and the Way Forward

Addressing Socio-Economic Barriers

To ensure equitable access to education, it is essential to address socio-economic barriers that disproportionately affect girls. This includes providing financial support, scholarships, and incentives for families to prioritize girls' education. Policies that promote affordable and accessible education, such as free school meals and transportation, can also mitigate the impact of poverty on educational attainment.

Challenging Cultural Norms and Practices

Efforts to challenge and change cultural norms and practices that hinder girls' education are crucial. Community-based programs that engage parents, religious leaders, and local authorities can help shift attitudes and promote the value of educating girls. Advocacy campaigns and public awareness initiatives play a vital role in challenging stereotypes and promoting gender equality in education.

Investing in Infrastructure and Resources

Investing in educational infrastructure and resources, particularly in rural and underserved areas, is essential to ensure all girls have access to quality education. This includes building schools, providing safe and sanitary facilities, and ensuring access to learning materials and technology. Training and supporting teachers to deliver gender-sensitive and inclusive education is also critical.

Promoting Peace and Stability

Conflict and crisis situations pose significant challenges to girls' education. Promoting peace and stability, addressing the root causes of conflict, and ensuring the protection of educational institutions are essential for safeguarding girls' right to education. Humanitarian efforts should prioritize education in emergency response plans and provide safe learning environments for children affected by conflict.

Conclusion

Education is a powerful catalyst for advancing women's rights and achieving gender equality. While significant progress has been made, substantial disparities in access to education for girls and women persist. Addressing these disparities and promoting equitable access to quality education is essential for empowering women, fostering economic growth, improving health outcomes, and driving social change.

As we continue to explore the history and impact of women's rights, it is clear that education plays a central role in transforming lives and communities. The stories of women and girls who have overcome barriers to education and achieved remarkable success serve as a testament to the enduring power of education in advancing gender equality and empowering future generations.

Chapter 6
Women's Health and Reproductive Rights

Introduction

Women's health and reproductive rights have been pivotal issues in the fight for gender equality. The ability to control their own reproductive health is fundamental to women's autonomy, affecting their physical health, economic stability, and social standing. This chapter delves into the history and ongoing struggle for women's health and reproductive rights, focusing on key topics such as birth control, abortion rights, and access to healthcare. We will explore significant legal battles, global disparities, and the persistent challenges faced by women in different parts of the world.

Birth Control: A Revolutionary Advancement

Early Contraceptive Methods

For centuries, women sought ways to control their fertility using a variety of often unreliable and unsafe methods. Traditional birth control methods included herbal remedies, barrier methods like diaphragms and condoms, and practices such as withdrawal and abstinence. However, these methods were largely ineffective and lacked scientific backing.

The Birth Control Movement

The modern birth control movement began in the early 20th century, spearheaded by activists like Margaret Sanger. Sanger, a nurse and social reformer, opened the first birth control clinic in the United States in 1916 and later founded the organization that became Planned Parenthood. She advocated for women's right to access contraceptive information and methods, challenging laws that prohibited the dissemination of birth control information.

The Pill and Its Impact

The introduction of the oral contraceptive pill in the 1960s revolutionized women's reproductive health. The Pill provided a reliable and convenient method of birth control, granting women greater control over their reproductive lives. It contributed to the sexual revolution, allowing women to engage in sexual activity without the constant fear of unwanted pregnancy. The Pill also had significant social and economic impacts, enabling women to pursue higher education and careers without interruption.

Abortion Rights: A Contentious Battle

Historical Context

Abortion has been practiced for millennia, but its legality and social acceptance have fluctuated over time. In the 19th and early 20th centuries, many countries criminalized abortion, forcing women to seek unsafe and illegal procedures. The dangers associated with illegal abortions prompted a movement for reproductive rights and the legalization of abortion.

Roe v. Wade

One of the most significant legal victories for reproductive rights was the U.S. Supreme Court's decision in Roe v. Wade in 1973. The Court ruled that a woman's right to choose to have an abortion was protected under the constitutional right to privacy. This landmark decision legalized abortion nationwide, reducing the number of unsafe abortions and affirming women's autonomy over their reproductive health.

Global Perspectives

The legality and accessibility of abortion vary widely across the world. In some countries, such as Canada and much of Western Europe, abortion is widely accessible and viewed as a fundamental right. In contrast, many countries in Latin America, Africa, and parts of Asia have restrictive abortion laws, often only permitting the procedure in cases of rape, incest, or danger to the woman's life. These restrictions force many women to seek unsafe and illegal abortions, putting their health and lives at risk.

Access to Healthcare: A Critical Issue

Barriers to Healthcare

Access to comprehensive healthcare is crucial for women's health and well-being. However, women around the world face numerous barriers to healthcare, including:

Economic Barriers:

High costs of healthcare services and lack of insurance coverage prevent many women from accessing necessary care.

Geographic Barriers:

Women in rural and remote areas often lack access to healthcare facilities and providers.

Cultural and Social Barriers:

Cultural norms and gender discrimination can prevent women from seeking care or receiving appropriate treatment.

Legal Barriers:

Restrictive laws and policies, particularly around reproductive health services, limit women's access to essential healthcare.

Maternal Health

Maternal health is a critical component of women's healthcare. While significant progress has been made in reducing maternal mortality rates, disparities persist, particularly in low- and middle-income countries. Factors contributing to maternal mortality include lack of access to prenatal and postnatal care, skilled birth attendants, and emergency obstetric services. Efforts to improve maternal health focus on increasing access to quality care, education, and resources for women and healthcare providers.

Sexual and Reproductive Health Services

Comprehensive sexual and reproductive health services include family planning, contraception, safe abortion, and treatment for sexually transmitted infections (STIs). Access to these services is essential for women to maintain their health and exercise their reproductive rights. Advocacy and policy efforts aim to ensure that these services are available, affordable, and accessible to all women, regardless of their socio-economic status or geographic location.

Significant Legal Battles and Advocacy Efforts

Griswold v. Connecticut

The 1965 U.S. Supreme Court case Griswold v. Connecticut was a landmark decision that established the right to privacy in marital relations. The Court struck down a Connecticut law that prohibited the use of contraceptives, recognizing married couples' right to access birth control. This decision laid the groundwork for later reproductive rights cases, including Roe v. Wade.

Planned Parenthood v. Casey

In 1992, the U.S. Supreme Court case Planned Parenthood v. Casey reaffirmed the core holding of Roe v. Wade but allowed states to impose certain restrictions on abortion, as long as they did not place an "undue burden" on women seeking the procedure. This decision has led to a patchwork of state laws regulating abortion, with varying degrees of accessibility across the United States.

Global Advocacy and Movements

Global advocacy efforts have played a crucial role in advancing women's health and reproductive rights. Organizations such as the International Planned Parenthood Federation (IPPF), the Guttmacher Institute, and UN Women work to promote reproductive health, advocate for policy changes, and provide essential services to women worldwide. Movements like #MyBodyMyChoice and the International Women's Health Coalition (IWHC) continue to fight for women's rights and access to healthcare.

Ongoing Challenges and Future Directions

Addressing Inequities

Despite progress, significant inequities in women's health and reproductive rights persist. Efforts to address these inequities must focus on:

Improving Access: Expanding access to healthcare services, particularly in underserved and marginalized communities.

Education and Awareness: Increasing awareness and education about reproductive health and rights.

Policy and Advocacy:

Advocating for policies that protect and promote women's health and reproductive rights at local, national, and international levels.

Combatting Stigma and Discrimination

Stigma and discrimination surrounding women's reproductive health and rights remain significant barriers. Efforts to combat these issues include:

Public Awareness Campaigns:

Promoting positive attitudes toward reproductive health and rights.

Community Engagement:

Involving communities in discussions about reproductive health and addressing cultural and social norms that perpetuate stigma.

Legal Protections:

Ensuring legal protections against discrimination and violence related to reproductive health.

Innovation and Research

Innovation and research are essential for advancing women's health and reproductive rights. Areas of focus include:

Developing New Contraceptives:

Creating more effective, affordable, and accessible contraceptive methods.

Improving Maternal Health:

Researching and implementing best practices for maternal health care.

Addressing Emerging Health Issues:

Responding to emerging health issues, such as Zika virus and COVID-19, that disproportionately affect women.

Conclusion

The fight for women's health and reproductive rights is a crucial aspect of the broader struggle for gender equality. While significant progress has been made, ongoing challenges and disparities remain. Addressing these issues requires a multifaceted approach, including policy and legal reforms, education and awareness campaigns, and efforts to combat stigma and discrimination.

As we continue to explore the history and impact of women's rights, it is clear that access to comprehensive healthcare and the ability to make informed decisions about one's reproductive health are fundamental to women's empowerment and well-being. The stories of women and activists who have fought for these rights serve as a testament to the importance of continued advocacy and action in the pursuit of gender equality.

Chapter 7
Violence Against Women

Introduction

Violence against women is a pervasive and deeply entrenched issue that affects women globally, cutting across boundaries of age, race, socio-economic status, and geography. This chapter addresses the various forms of violence against women, including domestic violence, sexual assault, and human trafficking. We will explore the impact of this violence on individuals and societies, highlight initiatives and organizations working to combat these issues, and support survivors, and discuss ongoing challenges in eradicating violence against women.

Forms of Violence Against Women

Domestic Violence

Domestic violence, also known as intimate partner violence (IPV), includes physical, sexual, emotional, and psychological abuse by a current or former partner or spouse. It is a pattern of behavior used to gain or maintain power and control over an intimate partner.

Physical Abuse:

Hitting, slapping, punching, choking, and other forms of physical harm.

Sexual Abuse:

Coercing or attempting to coerce any sexual contact without consent.

Emotional Abuse:

Undermining an individual's sense of self-worth through constant criticism, name-calling, or damaging relationships with others.

Psychological Abuse:

Instilling fear through intimidation, threatening physical harm, destruction of property, or forced isolation.

Sexual Assault

Sexual assault refers to any non-consensual sexual act, including rape, attempted rape, molestation, and other forms of sexual violence. It can occur in various settings, including within relationships, at home, in the workplace, and in public spaces.

Rape:

Non-consensual penetration, whether vaginal, anal, or oral.

Molestation:

Unwanted touching or fondling.

Sexual Harassment:

Unwanted sexual advances, requests for sexual favors, and other verbal or physical harassment of a sexual nature.

Human Trafficking

Human trafficking involves the recruitment, transportation, transfer, harboring, or receipt of individuals through force, fraud, or coercion for the purpose of exploitation. Women and girls are disproportionately affected by human trafficking, often being trafficked for sexual exploitation and forced labor.

Sex Trafficking:

Coercing or deceiving individuals into commercial sex acts.

Labor Trafficking:

Forcing individuals to work under threat or coercion, often in inhumane conditions and for little or no pay.

Impact of Violence Against Women

Physical and Mental Health

Violence against women has profound and lasting effects on physical and mental health. Survivors may experience chronic pain, gastrointestinal disorders, gynecological problems, and a range of psychological issues such as depression, anxiety, post-traumatic stress disorder (PTSD), and suicidal tendencies.

Social and Economic Costs

The social and economic costs of violence against women are significant. Survivors may face stigma and social isolation, impacting their ability to maintain relationships and participate in community life. Economically, violence can lead to loss of income due to missed work, medical expenses, and decreased productivity, which in turn affects families and broader communities.

Intergenerational Effects

Children who witness domestic violence are at risk of developing behavioral and emotional problems, experiencing abuse themselves, and perpetuating the cycle of violence in their own relationships. Addressing violence against women is crucial not only for the immediate survivors but also for breaking the cycle of violence for future generations.

Initiatives and Organizations Combatting Violence

International Frameworks and Agreements

Several international frameworks and agreements provide a basis for action against violence against women:

The Convention on the Elimination of All Forms of Discrimination Against Women (CEDAW):

An international treaty adopted by the United Nations General Assembly that defines what constitutes discrimination against women and sets up an agenda for national action to end such discrimination.

The Declaration on the Elimination of Violence Against Women:

Adopted by the UN General Assembly in 1993, this declaration recognizes violence against women as a violation of human rights and calls for national and international measures to eliminate it.

The Istanbul Convention:

The Council of Europe Convention on preventing and combating violence against women and domestic violence, which aims to protect women against all forms of violence and prevent, prosecute, and eliminate violence against women and domestic violence.

Key Organizations

Numerous organizations at the international, national, and local levels work to combat violence against women and support survivors:

UN Women:

A United Nations entity dedicated to gender equality and the empowerment of women, UN Women supports international efforts to eliminate violence against women through advocacy, policy development, and on-the-ground initiatives.

The International Rescue Committee (IRC):

Provides emergency aid and long-term assistance to refugees and those displaced by war, persecution, or natural disaster. The IRC runs programs to support survivors of gender-based violence.

RAINN (Rape, Abuse & Incest National Network):

The largest anti-sexual violence organization in the United States, RAINN operates the National Sexual Assault Hotline and carries out programs to prevent sexual violence, help survivors, and ensure perpetrators are brought to justice.

The Global Network of Women's Shelters:

An international network that connects and supports shelters for women and children experiencing violence, facilitating the exchange of knowledge and strategies to enhance services and advocacy efforts.

Notable Initiatives

The #MeToo Movement:

A global movement that began in 2017 to expose the prevalence of sexual assault and harassment, particularly in the workplace. The movement has led to increased awareness, policy changes, and greater support for survivors.

The White Ribbon Campaign:

A global movement of men and boys working to end male violence against women. Participants wear white ribbons as a pledge to never commit, condone, or remain silent about violence against women.

Safe Cities and Safe Public Spaces:

An initiative by UN Women aimed at creating safer urban environments for women and girls through comprehensive strategies that address violence in public spaces.

Ongoing Challenges

Legal and Policy Gaps

In many countries, laws and policies related to violence against women are inadequate or poorly enforced. Some regions lack specific legislation criminalizing domestic violence or marital rape, while others have legal frameworks that are not effectively implemented. Strengthening legal protections and ensuring rigorous enforcement is essential for safeguarding women's rights.

Cultural and Social Norms

Deeply entrenched cultural and social norms often perpetuate violence against women. Traditional gender roles, societal acceptance of violence, and victim-blaming attitudes hinder progress. Changing these norms requires sustained efforts in education, community engagement, and public awareness campaigns.

Access to Services

Survivors of violence often face barriers to accessing essential services, including legal assistance, healthcare, and safe shelters. These barriers can be due to geographic location, lack of resources, or social stigma. Ensuring that services are accessible, affordable, and sensitive to the needs of survivors is crucial.

Intersectionality

Women from marginalized groups, including those based on race, ethnicity, sexual orientation, disability, and socio-economic status, often face compounded forms of violence and discrimination. Addressing violence against women requires an intersectional approach that recognizes and addresses these overlapping forms of oppression.

Case Studies

Rwanda: Post-Genocide Recovery

After the 1994 genocide, Rwanda faced significant challenges in addressing violence against women. The government and civil society organizations implemented comprehensive measures to support survivors and prevent future violence, including legal reforms, community-based programs, and initiatives to promote women's leadership and participation in decision-making. These efforts have contributed to significant progress in reducing violence and empowering women.

India: The Nirbhaya Case

The 2012 gang-rape and murder of a young woman in Delhi, known as the Nirbhaya case, sparked nationwide protests and led to significant legal and policy changes in India. The Criminal Law (Amendment) Act, 2013, introduced stricter penalties for sexual violence and established new legal provisions to protect women. The case also highlighted the need for societal change and greater awareness of gender-based violence.

Sweden: Comprehensive Approach to Domestic Violence

Sweden has implemented a comprehensive approach to addressing domestic violence, combining legal measures, support services, and public education. The Swedish government has enacted robust laws against domestic violence, funded shelters and support programs for survivors, and launched campaigns to change societal attitudes towards violence. This holistic approach has made Sweden a leader in efforts to combat domestic violence.

Conclusion

Violence against women is a profound violation of human rights that requires concerted and sustained efforts to eradicate. While significant progress has been made through legal reforms, advocacy, and support services, much work remains to be done. Addressing violence against women necessitates a multifaceted approach that includes legal and policy changes, cultural and social transformation, and ensuring access to comprehensive services for survivors.

As we continue to explore the history and impact of women's rights, it is crucial to recognize the pervasive nature of violence against women and the importance of ongoing advocacy and action. By supporting survivors, challenging harmful norms, and implementing effective policies, we can move closer to a world where all women can live free from violence and fear.

Chapter 8
Women in Politics

Introduction

The increasing presence of women in politics marks a significant advancement in the quest for gender equality. Women's participation in political leadership not only enhances representation but also brings diverse perspectives to policy-making and governance. This chapter explores the historical and contemporary impact of women in politics, highlighting trailblazing figures like Indira Gandhi, Margaret Thatcher, Angela Merkel, and Jacinda Ardern. Their contributions demonstrate how women in political power can influence policy, governance, and societal change.

Historical Trailblazers

Indira Gandhi

Indira Gandhi, the first and only female Prime Minister of India, served from 1966 to 1977 and again from 1980 until her assassination in 1984. She was a central figure in Indian politics and played a crucial role in shaping the country's domestic and foreign policies.

Economic Policies:

Gandhi's tenure saw significant economic reforms, including the nationalization of banks and the promotion of the Green Revolution, which aimed to increase agricultural productivity and self-sufficiency in food grains.

Emergency Rule:

Her controversial decision to declare a state of emergency from 1975 to 1977, suspending constitutional rights and arresting political opponents, remains a contentious period in India's democratic history. This period highlighted the complexities and challenges of her leadership.

Foreign Policy:

Gandhi strengthened India's position on the global stage, notably through the 1971 Indo-Pakistani War, which led to the creation of Bangladesh. Her leadership demonstrated a blend of assertiveness and strategic diplomacy.

Margaret Thatcher

Margaret Thatcher, the first female Prime Minister of the United Kingdom, served from 1979 to 1990. Known as the "Iron Lady," she was a dominant force in British and global politics during her tenure.

Economic Reforms:

Thatcher implemented a series of neoliberal economic policies, including privatization of state-owned industries, deregulation, and reduction of trade union power. Her approach aimed to reduce government intervention and stimulate economic growth but also led to significant social and economic disparities.

Foreign Policy:

Thatcher was a staunch ally of the United States during the Cold War and played a key role in the Falklands War, asserting British sovereignty over the Falkland Islands. Her strong stance on international issues cemented her reputation as a formidable leader.

Legacy:

While her policies remain divisive, Thatcher's impact on British politics and her role as a pioneering female leader are undeniable. She broke the glass ceiling and set a precedent for women in political leadership.

Contemporary Leaders

Angela Merkel

Angela Merkel, the first female Chancellor of Germany, served from 2005 to 2021. Her pragmatic and steady leadership earned her the nickname "Mutti" (Mother) and established her as one of the world's most influential leaders.

Economic Stability:

Merkel's tenure is marked by strong economic management, particularly during the Eurozone crisis. Her policies helped maintain Germany's economic stability and solidified its position as Europe's economic powerhouse.

Refugee Crisis:

In 2015, Merkel made the bold decision to open Germany's borders to refugees fleeing conflict in Syria and other regions. Her stance was both praised for its humanitarianism and criticized for its political and social challenges.

Climate Policy:

Merkel, a trained physicist, prioritized environmental issues and pushed for the transition to renewable energy, known as the Energiewende. Her commitment to combating climate change influenced global environmental policy.

Jacinda Ardern

Jacinda Ardern, the Prime Minister of New Zealand since 2017, is known for her compassionate and progressive leadership style. She has garnered international acclaim for her handling of various crises and her focus on social issues.

Crisis Management:

Ardern's leadership during the Christchurch mosque shootings in 2019 and the COVID-19 pandemic showcased her empathetic and decisive approach. Her response to the shootings included swift action on gun control and a unifying message of solidarity.

Social Policies:

Ardern has championed policies aimed at reducing child poverty, improving mental health services, and addressing housing affordability. Her focus on social justice and well-being reflects a commitment to inclusive governance.

International Impact:

Ardern's progressive and empathetic leadership has set a new standard for political leaders globally. Her emphasis on kindness and community has resonated beyond New Zealand's borders, influencing political discourse worldwide.

The Impact of Women in Politics

Policy and Governance

Women in political leadership bring unique perspectives and priorities to policy-making. Research shows that female politicians are more likely to advocate for social issues such as healthcare, education, and family welfare. Their presence often leads to more comprehensive and inclusive policies.

Health and Education:

Female leaders tend to prioritize healthcare and education, leading to improved outcomes in these sectors. For example, Rwanda, with a majority female parliament, has made significant strides in healthcare and education.

Gender Equality:

Women in politics often champion gender equality initiatives, including legislation to combat gender-based violence, promote equal pay, and ensure reproductive rights. Their advocacy is crucial for advancing women's rights globally.

Peace and Security:

Studies indicate that women's participation in peace processes contributes to more durable and comprehensive peace agreements. Female leaders often emphasize dialogue, reconciliation, and social cohesion in conflict resolution.

Representation and Inspiration

The presence of women in political leadership serves as a powerful symbol of gender equality and inspires future generations of women to pursue careers in politics and leadership. It challenges traditional gender roles and encourages societies to value diverse leadership styles.

Role Models:

Women like Merkel, Ardern, Gandhi, and Thatcher serve as role models, demonstrating that women can lead effectively in various political and cultural contexts. Their success stories inspire young women to aspire to leadership roles.

Breaking Stereotypes:

Female political leaders challenge stereotypes about women's capabilities and leadership styles. Their success underscores the importance of diversity and inclusion in governance.

Challenges and Barriers

Despite significant progress, women in politics continue to face numerous challenges and barriers:

Gender Bias and Discrimination:

Female politicians often encounter gender bias and discrimination, including sexist attitudes, media scrutiny, and unequal treatment compared to their male counterparts.

Violence and Harassment:

Women in politics are disproportionately subjected to violence and harassment, both online and offline. This can deter women from entering or remaining in political careers.

Balancing Roles:

Women in political leadership often juggle multiple roles and responsibilities, facing societal expectations related to family and caregiving. This dual burden can be a significant barrier to their political engagement and success.

Initiatives to Promote Women in Politics

Quotas and Affirmative Action

Many countries have implemented gender quotas and affirmative action policies to increase women's representation in politics. These measures have proven effective in enhancing gender diversity in political institutions.

Rwanda:

Rwanda's constitution mandates a minimum of 30% women in decision-making bodies. As a result, Rwanda has one of the highest percentages of women in parliament globally, with women holding over 60% of seats.

Scandinavia:

Countries like Norway and Sweden have implemented voluntary party quotas, leading to high levels of female representation in their parliaments.

Capacity Building and Mentorship

Programs aimed at building the capacity of women to run for office and succeed in political careers are crucial. These programs offer training, mentorship, and support networks for aspiring female politicians.

EMILY's List:

In the United States, EMILY's List works to elect pro-choice Democratic women to office. The organization provides training, financial support, and resources for female candidates.

UN Women Initiatives:

UN Women supports various initiatives worldwide to empower women in politics, including leadership training programs and advocacy for gender-sensitive policies.

Conclusion

The increasing presence of women in politics represents a significant step towards gender equality and inclusive governance. Trailblazing leaders like Indira Gandhi, Margaret Thatcher, Angela Merkel, and Jacinda Ardern have demonstrated the profound impact women can have on policy and governance. Their contributions highlight the importance of diverse leadership and the need for continued efforts to overcome barriers and challenges.

As we continue to explore the history and impact of women's rights, it is clear that women's political participation is essential for creating more equitable and just societies. By promoting gender equality in political leadership, we can ensure that the voices and perspectives of all citizens are represented in the halls of power.

Chapter 9
Intersectionality in the Women's Rights Movement

Introduction

Intersectionality is a crucial concept in understanding the complexities of women's experiences and the multifaceted nature of oppression. Coined by Kimberlé Crenshaw in 1989, intersectionality refers to the interconnectedness of social categorizations such as race, class, and sexuality, which create overlapping systems of discrimination and disadvantage. This chapter introduces the concept of intersectionality, explores how various factors intersect with gender to shape women's lives, and highlights the importance of inclusive feminism that amplifies the voices of marginalized women.

The Concept of Intersectionality

Origins and Definition

Intersectionality emerged from the need to address the limitations of traditional feminist frameworks that often overlooked the diverse experiences of women, particularly women of color. Kimberlé Crenshaw, a legal scholar and civil rights advocate, introduced the term to explain how race and gender intersect to impact the lives of African American women in unique ways.

Definition:

Intersectionality is the theory that various social identities (e.g., race, gender, sexuality, class) interact to create specific experiences of oppression and privilege. These interactions are not merely additive but produce unique and compounded forms of discrimination.

Purpose:

The concept aims to reveal the multifaceted nature of social inequalities and advocate for more nuanced and inclusive approaches to social justice.

Intersectionality in Feminism

Traditional feminist movements often centered on the experiences of white, middle-class women, thereby marginalizing women of color, working-class women, LGBTQ+ individuals, and others with intersecting identities. Intersectionality calls for an inclusive feminism that recognizes and addresses the diverse realities of all women.

How Intersectionality Shapes Women's Experiences

Race and Gender

Women of color face unique challenges that differ from those of white women due to the combined effects of racism and sexism.

Workplace Discrimination:

Women of color are more likely to experience discrimination in hiring, promotion, and pay compared to their white counterparts. This double burden of racism and sexism limits their economic opportunities and career advancement.

Healthcare Inequality:

Racial disparities in healthcare mean that women of color often receive lower quality care and face higher rates of maternal mortality and morbidity. Structural racism within the healthcare system exacerbates these issues.

Class and Gender

Socio-economic status significantly impacts women's experiences, influencing their access to resources, opportunities, and quality of life.

Economic Inequality:

Women from lower socio-economic backgrounds face higher levels of poverty, job insecurity, and inadequate housing. Economic policies and labor practices often fail to address the specific needs of poor and working-class women.

Education:

Access to education is crucial for economic mobility, yet women from low-income families often encounter barriers to obtaining quality education. These barriers include financial constraints, lack of supportive services, and systemic inequalities in educational institutions.

Sexuality and Gender

LGBTQ+ women experience discrimination and violence based on both their gender and sexual orientation.

Social Stigma and Violence:

Lesbian, bisexual, and transgender women face higher risks of violence, including hate crimes and intimate partner violence. Social stigma and discrimination in healthcare, employment, and housing further marginalize LGBTQ+ women.

Legal Rights and Protections:

Legal systems in many countries fail to protect LGBTQ+ individuals adequately, leaving them vulnerable to discrimination and exclusion. Advocacy for inclusive legal frameworks is essential to ensure their rights and safety.

Disability and Gender

Women with disabilities encounter unique barriers and forms of discrimination that intersect with their gender.

Accessibility:

Physical, attitudinal, and systemic barriers limit the participation of women with disabilities in various aspects of life, including education, employment, and social activities.

Healthcare Disparities:

Women with disabilities often face challenges in accessing appropriate healthcare services. These challenges include lack of accessible facilities, inadequate training of healthcare providers, and discriminatory attitudes.

Inclusive Feminism

Recognizing Diverse Experiences

Inclusive feminism emphasizes the importance of acknowledging and valuing the diverse experiences and identities of all women. This approach seeks to dismantle the hierarchies within feminist movements and advocate for the rights of the most marginalized.

Amplifying Marginalized Voices:

Inclusive feminism prioritizes the voices and leadership of women who have historically been marginalized within feminist movements, including women of color, LGBTQ+ women, disabled women, and women from low-income backgrounds.

Solidarity and Allyship:

Building solidarity across different identities and experiences is essential for a more effective and united feminist movement. Allyship involves listening to, supporting, and advocating alongside marginalized communities.

Intersectional Activism

Intersectional activism addresses the interconnected nature of social injustices and advocates for comprehensive solutions that consider multiple dimensions of identity.

Policy Advocacy:

Intersectional activists work to influence policies that address the root causes of inequality and oppression, such as systemic racism, economic injustice, and discriminatory practices. This includes advocating for equitable healthcare, education, and labor policies.

Community-Based Approaches:

Grassroots organizations and community-based initiatives play a vital role in addressing intersectional issues. These approaches are often more responsive to the specific needs of marginalized communities and can drive meaningful change from the ground up.

Voices of Marginalized Women

Historical Figures

Sojourner Truth:

An African American abolitionist and women's rights activist, Sojourner Truth highlighted the intersections of race and gender in her famous "Ain't I a Woman?" speech. She challenged both racial and gender inequalities, advocating for the rights of Black women and all oppressed individuals.

Audre Lorde:

A Black lesbian feminist, poet, and activist, Audre Lorde emphasized the importance of recognizing and embracing the differences among women. Her writings and activism called for a more inclusive and intersectional approach to feminism.

Contemporary Leaders

Tarana Burke:

The founder of the #MeToo movement, Tarana Burke has been a leading voice in advocating for survivors of sexual violence, particularly women of color. Her work emphasizes the need to center the experiences of marginalized women in discussions about sexual violence and justice.

Laverne Cox:

An actress and transgender rights activist, Laverne Cox has been a prominent advocate for transgender women, particularly those of color. Her activism highlights the unique challenges faced by transgender individuals and calls for greater inclusion and equality.

Case Studies

Black Lives Matter and Intersectional Feminism

The Black Lives Matter (BLM) movement, founded by Alicia Garza, Patrisse Cullors, and Opal Tometi, exemplifies intersectional activism. While BLM primarily addresses police brutality and systemic racism against Black people, it also emphasizes the importance of intersectionality by advocating for the rights of Black women, LGBTQ+ individuals, and other marginalized groups within the Black community.

The Women's March

The Women's March, first held in 2017, brought millions of people together to advocate for women's rights and social justice. The movement's leadership and platform embraced intersectionality by addressing issues such as racial justice, LGBTQ+ rights, environmental justice, and economic inequality. The Women's March highlighted the need for a broad and inclusive feminist agenda.

Ongoing Challenges

Addressing Internal Biases

Even within feminist movements, internal biases and exclusionary practices can persist. Addressing these issues requires ongoing self-reflection, education, and commitment to inclusivity.

Privilege and Power Dynamics:

Recognizing and challenging privilege within feminist spaces is essential for creating more inclusive movements. This includes examining how power dynamics can marginalize certain voices and working to redistribute power more equitably.

Intersectional Education:

Educating feminist activists and allies about intersectionality and the diverse experiences of women is crucial for fostering empathy, understanding, and effective advocacy.

Building Inclusive Movements

Building inclusive feminist movements involves creating spaces where all women feel valued, heard, and supported. This requires intentional efforts to dismantle barriers to participation and ensure that marginalized voices are central to the movement.

Inclusive Leadership:

Promoting diverse leadership within feminist organizations and movements ensures that different perspectives and experiences are represented in decision-making processes.

Collaborative Approaches:

Collaboration across different social justice movements can strengthen intersectional activism. Building alliances with organizations and movements focused on racial justice, LGBTQ+ rights, disability rights, and economic justice can enhance the impact of feminist advocacy.

Conclusion

Intersectionality is a vital framework for understanding and addressing the complex and interconnected forms of oppression that women face. By embracing inclusive feminism and amplifying the voices of marginalized women, the women's rights movement can more effectively advocate for justice and equality for all women.

As we continue to explore the history and impact of women's rights, it is essential to recognize the diverse experiences and identities that shape women's lives. An intersectional approach to feminism not only enriches our understanding of gender inequality but also strengthens our collective efforts to create a more just and equitable world.

Chapter 10
The Role of Men in Advancing Women's Rights

Introduction

The advancement of women's rights is not solely a women's issue; it requires the active participation and support of men as well. Recognizing the role of men as allies in the feminist movement is crucial for achieving gender equality. This chapter examines the importance of male involvement in supporting women's rights, highlights notable male allies in history and contemporary society, and discusses the concept of gender partnership as a vital component in the fight for equality.

The Importance of Male Involvement

Challenging Patriarchy and Gender Norms

Patriarchy, a system in which men hold primary power and dominate in roles of political leadership, moral authority, social privilege, and control of property, perpetuates gender inequality. For significant progress to be made in dismantling patriarchy, men must actively challenge and reject these power structures.

Redefining Masculinity:

Traditional notions of masculinity often promote dominance, aggression, and emotional suppression. Encouraging men to embrace a broader, healthier range of masculinities can reduce harmful behaviors and foster more equitable relationships.

Role Models:

Men who advocate for gender equality serve as role models, demonstrating that supporting women's rights is compatible with being a strong, compassionate, and ethical individual.

Shared Benefits of Gender Equality

Gender equality benefits everyone, not just women. Men also stand to gain from a more equitable society.

Improved Relationships:

Gender equality fosters healthier, more respectful relationships between men and women. It promotes mutual respect and understanding, reducing conflict and enhancing emotional well-being.

Economic Advantages:

Gender equality can boost economic growth. When women participate fully in the workforce, economies thrive. Men benefit from more robust economic systems and diverse workplaces.

Social Progress:

Societies that promote gender equality tend to be more just, stable, and peaceful. Men, as members of these societies, enjoy the benefits of living in a more equitable and harmonious environment.

Male Allies in the Feminist Movement

Historical Figures

Frederick Douglass:

An African American abolitionist and former enslaved person, Frederick Douglass was a staunch advocate for women's rights. He attended the Seneca Falls Convention in 1848 and supported the suffrage movement, emphasizing the interconnectedness of the struggles for racial and gender equality.

John Stuart Mill:

A British philosopher and political economist, John Stuart Mill wrote extensively on women's rights. His book "The Subjection of Women," published in 1869, argued for equality between the sexes and criticized the legal and social restrictions placed on women.

William Lloyd Garrison:

An abolitionist and social reformer, William Lloyd Garrison was a vocal supporter of women's suffrage. He believed in the fundamental equality of all people and advocated for the rights of women alongside his work to end slavery.

Contemporary Allies

Justin Trudeau:

As the Prime Minister of Canada, Justin Trudeau has been an outspoken advocate for gender equality. His commitment to appointing a gender-balanced cabinet in 2015 demonstrated his dedication to women's rights and set an example for other world leaders.

Barack Obama:

During his presidency, Barack Obama consistently supported women's rights, advocating for equal pay, reproductive rights, and measures to combat gender-based violence. He often spoke about the importance of gender equality in creating a just society.

HeForShe Campaign:

Launched by UN Women, the HeForShe campaign encourages men to take an active role in promoting gender equality. High-profile supporters, including actors, athletes, and political leaders, have helped raise awareness and mobilize men around the world to support women's rights.

Gender Partnership: A Collaborative Approach

Principles of Gender Partnership

Gender partnership involves men and women working together to achieve gender equality. It is based on mutual respect, collaboration, and the recognition that both genders have a stake in creating a more equitable world.

Mutual Respect:

Gender partnership requires acknowledging and valuing each other's contributions and perspectives. Men and women must listen to and learn from one another, fostering an environment of respect and cooperation.

Shared Responsibility:

Achieving gender equality is a shared responsibility. Men must recognize their role in perpetuating gender inequalities and take proactive steps to address and dismantle these systems.

Collaborative Action:

Effective gender partnership involves collaborative action. Men and women must work together in various spheres—home, workplace, and community—to promote and implement policies and practices that support gender equality.

Strategies for Engaging Men

Successfully engaging men in the fight for gender equality requires targeted strategies that address their unique perspectives and challenges.

Education and Awareness:

Raising awareness about gender inequality and its impact on both women and men is essential. Educational programs and campaigns can help men understand the importance of gender equality and inspire them to become advocates.

Positive Reinforcement:

Highlighting positive examples of male allies and showcasing the benefits of gender equality can motivate men to get involved. Celebrating men who actively support women's rights reinforces the idea that gender equality is a collective goal.

Creating Safe Spaces:

Providing safe spaces for men to discuss gender issues and express their concerns can facilitate open dialogue and mutual understanding. Men need opportunities to explore their own experiences with gender norms and learn how they can contribute to change.

Case Studies

The White Ribbon Campaign

The White Ribbon Campaign, founded in 1991 in Canada, is one of the largest movements of men and boys working to end violence against women and girls. It encourages men to take a stand against gender-based violence and promotes healthy, respectful relationships.

Educational Programs:

The campaign offers educational programs in schools, workplaces, and communities to raise awareness about gender-based violence and promote gender equality.

Public Advocacy:

White Ribbon advocates for policy changes that address violence against women and supports initiatives that promote gender equality.

MenEngage Alliance

The MenEngage Alliance is a global network of organizations and activists working to engage men and boys in promoting gender equality and preventing gender-based violence.

Community Engagement:

The alliance works with communities around the world to challenge harmful gender norms and promote positive masculinity. It emphasizes the importance of local solutions and cultural context in addressing gender inequality.

Policy Advocacy:

MenEngage advocates for policies that support gender equality, including those related to education, healthcare, and economic opportunities. It collaborates with governments, NGOs, and international organizations to influence policy change.

The Future of Gender Partnership

Transforming Social Norms

Achieving gender equality requires a fundamental shift in social norms and attitudes. Men play a crucial role in this transformation by challenging traditional gender roles and promoting values of equality and respect.

Media and Representation:

Media and popular culture have a significant influence on shaping social norms. Promoting diverse and positive representations of men who support gender equality can help change public perceptions and encourage more men to get involved.

Intergenerational Change:

Engaging young men and boys in discussions about gender equality from an early age can create lasting change. Educational programs that promote gender sensitivity and respect for all individuals are essential for fostering a culture of equality.

Sustaining Momentum

Sustaining momentum in the fight for gender equality requires ongoing commitment and action from both men and women.

Continued Advocacy:

Advocacy efforts must continue to push for policy changes and social reforms that support gender equality. Men can play a vital role in advocating for these changes within their communities, workplaces, and governments.

Building Alliances:

Building strong alliances between men's and women's organizations can enhance the impact of gender equality initiatives. Collaborative efforts that leverage the strengths and resources of diverse groups can drive more effective and sustainable change.

Conclusion

The role of men in advancing women's rights is indispensable. As allies and partners, men can contribute to dismantling patriarchal structures, challenging harmful gender norms, and promoting a more inclusive and equitable society. Recognizing the shared benefits of gender equality and fostering gender partnership are essential steps in achieving lasting change.

By working together, men and women can create a world where gender equality is the norm, not the exception. As we continue to explore the history and impact of women's rights, it is clear that the active involvement of men is crucial for building a more just and equitable future for all.

Chapter 11
Women and the Media

Introduction

The media plays a pivotal role in shaping societal attitudes and perceptions. The portrayal of women in media—ranging from television and film to news and social media—significantly influences how women are viewed and treated in society. This chapter analyzes the depiction of women in various forms of media, the impact of these portrayals on societal attitudes, the progress made in achieving accurate and fair representation, and the influential women who have shaped public discourse through their work in media.

Historical Depictions of Women in Media

Early Media Representations

In the early 20th century, women in media were often portrayed in limited and stereotypical roles. These portrayals reflected and reinforced the societal norms and expectations of the time.

Silent Film Era:

Women were frequently cast as damsels in distress or as the object of male desire. Their roles were largely passive, with little agency or complexity.

Golden Age of Hollywood:

While this era saw the rise of iconic actresses, women were often confined to roles that emphasized their beauty and romantic appeal, rather than their intellectual or professional capabilities.

Mid-20th Century to 1980s

The mid-20th century brought some changes, but many stereotypes persisted.

Domesticity and Femininity:

Television programs often depicted women as housewives and mothers, reinforcing traditional gender roles. Shows like "Leave it to Beaver" and "The Donna Reed Show" epitomized this trend.

Sexualization:

In both film and advertising, women were frequently sexualized, with their value often tied to their physical appearance and attractiveness.

Impact of Media Portrayals on Society

Stereotypes and Gender Norms

The media's portrayal of women contributes to the reinforcement of gender stereotypes and societal norms.

Gender Roles:

Media representations often perpetuate traditional gender roles, depicting women as caregivers, homemakers, or secondary to male characters. This can limit societal expectations of what women can achieve.

Body Image:

The media's focus on unrealistic beauty standards and sexualized images of women contributes to body image issues and unhealthy standards of beauty. This can lead to negative self-esteem and eating disorders among women and girls.

Influence on Attitudes and Behaviors

The way women are portrayed in media can influence societal attitudes and behaviors towards women.

Normalization of Violence:

Media portrayals that glamorize or trivialize violence against women can contribute to the normalization of such behavior. This can impact the way society views and responds to violence against women.

Empowerment and Aspiration:

Conversely, positive and diverse portrayals of women in media can inspire and empower women and girls. Seeing women in leadership roles, pursuing careers, and achieving personal goals can broaden the scope of what is seen as possible for women.

Progress in Media Representation

Breaking Stereotypes

Recent decades have seen significant progress in breaking down stereotypes and presenting more nuanced portrayals of women.

Complex Characters:

Television shows and films are increasingly featuring complex, multifaceted female characters. Shows like "The Good Wife," "Scandal," and "Killing Eve" highlight women in powerful, diverse roles.

Diverse Representation:

Efforts to increase diversity in media have led to better representation of women of different races, ethnicities, sexual orientations, and backgrounds. This has helped to challenge monolithic portrayals of women.

Influential Movements and Campaigns

Several movements and campaigns have been instrumental in advocating for better representation of women in media.

#MeToo Movement:

Originating as a social media campaign to highlight the prevalence of sexual harassment and assault, #MeToo has had a profound impact on the media industry. It has led to increased awareness and accountability, as well as more respectful and equitable portrayals of women.

#TimesUp:

This movement, launched by women in the entertainment industry, aims to combat systemic sexual harassment and promote gender equality. It has also focused on improving the representation of women in media.

Influential Women in Media

Pioneers and Trailblazers

Throughout history, many women have made significant contributions to media, shaping public discourse and challenging stereotypes.

Lucille Ball:

As the star and producer of "I Love Lucy," Lucille Ball broke new ground in television. She was one of the first women to own her own production company, Desilu Productions, and played a key role in the development of iconic TV shows.

Barbara Walters:

A trailblazing journalist, Barbara Walters became the first female co-anchor of a network evening news program in 1976. Her career in broadcast journalism paved the way for future generations of women in the field.

Contemporary Influences

In contemporary media, numerous women continue to shape public discourse and push for greater representation.

Oprah Winfrey:

As a media mogul, talk show host, and philanthropist, Oprah Winfrey has had a profound influence on media and culture. Her work has addressed a wide range of social issues, including gender equality and empowerment.

Shonda Rhimes:

As a prolific television producer and writer, Shonda Rhimes has created popular shows like "Grey's Anatomy" and "Scandal." Her work is known for its diverse casting and strong, complex female characters.

Ava DuVernay:

A filmmaker and producer, Ava DuVernay has made significant contributions to film and television. Her works, including "Selma" and "A Wrinkle in Time," focus on social justice and feature diverse casts and powerful female leads.

The Role of Social Media

Amplifying Voices

Social media has become a powerful platform for women to share their stories and advocate for change.

Activism and Advocacy:

Social media campaigns, such as #MeToo and #TimesUp, have raised awareness about issues affecting women and have mobilized support for gender equality.

Influencers and Content Creators:

Women influencers and content creators on platforms like Instagram, YouTube, and TikTok are using their platforms to challenge stereotypes, promote body positivity, and advocate for women's rights.

Challenges and Opportunities

While social media offers opportunities for empowerment, it also presents challenges.

Cyberbullying and Harassment:

Women often face harassment and abuse online, which can be a significant barrier to their participation and expression on social media.

Representation and Influence:

Social media can perpetuate harmful stereotypes and unrealistic standards, but it also has the potential to democratize media representation and give voice to diverse perspectives.

The Future of Women in Media

Continued Advocacy

Continued advocacy is essential to ensure that progress in media representation is sustained and expanded.

Media Literacy:

Promoting media literacy can help audiences critically analyze media portrayals and advocate for more accurate and fair representation.

Policy and Regulation:

Policies and regulations that promote diversity and inclusion in media production can drive systemic change. This includes measures to support women in media careers and ensure equitable representation.

Creating Inclusive Media

Creating inclusive media requires a concerted effort from all stakeholders in the media industry.

Diverse Voices:

Ensuring that women from diverse backgrounds have opportunities to tell their stories and contribute to media production is crucial. This includes hiring women in key roles such as directors, writers, producers, and executives.

Audience Engagement:

Engaging with diverse audiences and listening to their feedback can help media creators produce content that resonates with and represents a broad spectrum of experiences and perspectives.

Conclusion

The portrayal of women in media has evolved significantly over time, reflecting and influencing societal attitudes towards gender equality. While progress has been made in achieving more accurate and fair representation, challenges remain. The continued involvement of women in media production, the support of male allies, and the active engagement of audiences are essential for driving further change.

As we move forward, the role of media in shaping public discourse and societal norms cannot be overstated. By promoting diverse and empowering portrayals of women, media can contribute to a more equitable and just society, where women are seen and valued for their full range of abilities, experiences, and contributions.

Chapter 12
Women in Science and Technology

Introduction

The fields of science and technology have historically been dominated by men, but women have made significant contributions that have often been overlooked or undervalued. This chapter explores the achievements of pioneering women in science and technology, highlights contemporary efforts to encourage more women to pursue careers in STEM (Science, Technology, Engineering, and Mathematics), and examines the ongoing challenges and opportunities for women in these fields.

Historical Contributions of Women in Science and Technology

Pioneering Figures

Marie Curie (1867–1934)

Marie Curie was a physicist and chemist who conducted pioneering research on radioactivity. She was the first woman to win a Nobel Prize and remains the only person to have won Nobel Prizes in two different scientific fields: Physics (1903) and Chemistry (1911).

Key Achievements:

Curie discovered the elements polonium and radium, and her work laid the foundation for the development of X-ray machines.

Legacy:

Curie's groundbreaking research and her role as a trailblazer for women in science have inspired generations of female scientists.

Ada Lovelace (1815–1852)

Ada Lovelace is often considered the world's first computer programmer. She worked with Charles Babbage on his early mechanical general-purpose computer, the Analytical Engine.

Key Achievements:

Lovelace wrote the first algorithm intended to be carried out by a machine, anticipating the future role of computers in society.

Legacy:

Lovelace's vision of computing's potential and her contributions to early computer science have earned her recognition as a pioneer in the field.

Rosalind Franklin (1920–1958)

Rosalind Franklin was a chemist whose work with X-ray diffraction was crucial to the discovery of the DNA double helix structure.

Key Achievements:

Franklin's photographs of DNA, particularly Photo 51, provided key insights that led to the identification of the DNA structure by Watson and Crick.

Legacy:

Franklin's contributions to molecular biology have been increasingly recognized, highlighting the importance of acknowledging women's contributions in scientific discoveries.

Overlooked and Underappreciated Contributions

Throughout history, many women have made significant scientific contributions that were overlooked or attributed to their male colleagues. Efforts to rectify these oversights are essential in providing a more accurate historical record.

Lise Meitner:

A physicist who played a crucial role in the discovery of nuclear fission, her contributions were overshadowed by her collaborator Otto Hahn, who received the Nobel Prize for their joint work.

Jocelyn Bell Burnell:

An astrophysicist who discovered the first radio pulsars, but the Nobel Prize for this discovery was awarded to her male thesis advisor.

Contemporary Women in Science and Technology

Breaking Barriers

Women continue to break barriers in science and technology, achieving remarkable success and pushing the boundaries of their fields.

Katherine Johnson (1918–2020):

A mathematician whose calculations of orbital mechanics were critical to the success of the first U.S. crewed spaceflights. Her story gained widespread recognition through the book and film "Hidden Figures."

Jane Goodall:

A primatologist and anthropologist known for her groundbreaking work with chimpanzees, reshaping our understanding of primate behavior and human evolution.

Mae Jemison:

The first African American woman to travel in space, Mae Jemison's career as an astronaut and physician has inspired countless young women to pursue careers in STEM.

Leading Organizations and Innovations

Women are leading organizations and spearheading innovations in science and technology, contributing to advancements in diverse fields.

Frances Arnold:

A Nobel laureate in Chemistry (2018) for her work on the directed evolution of enzymes, Frances Arnold's research has significant implications for bioengineering and sustainability.

Jennifer Doudna:

A biochemist who co-developed CRISPR-Cas9, a revolutionary gene-editing technology that has transformed genetics and holds promise for curing genetic diseases.

Encouraging Women in STEM

Educational Initiatives

Promoting STEM education for girls and young women is crucial for increasing female representation in science and technology.

STEM Programs and Camps:

Programs such as Girls Who Code and Black Girls Code provide young women with hands-on experience in coding and technology, fostering interest and skills in these fields.

Scholarships and Grants:

Financial support through scholarships and grants specifically for women in STEM helps to reduce barriers to higher education and research opportunities.

Mentorship and Role Models

Mentorship and the visibility of female role models play a vital role in encouraging women to pursue and persist in STEM careers.

Mentorship Programs:

Organizations like the Association for Women in Science (AWIS) and Women in Technology International (WITI) offer mentorship programs that connect aspiring female scientists and engineers with experienced professionals.

Role Models:

Highlighting the achievements of women in STEM through media, conferences, and educational materials can inspire the next generation of female scientists and technologists.

Workplace Policies and Practices

Creating inclusive and supportive workplace environments is essential for retaining women in STEM careers.

Work-Life Balance:

Policies that support work-life balance, such as flexible working hours and parental leave, help to accommodate the diverse needs of women in STEM.

Diversity and Inclusion:

Initiatives that promote diversity and inclusion, including unconscious bias training and diversity hiring practices, contribute to a more equitable work environment.

Addressing Challenges and Barriers

Gender Bias and Stereotypes

Despite progress, gender bias and stereotypes persist in STEM fields, presenting significant challenges for women.

Implicit Bias:

Implicit biases can affect hiring, promotion, and evaluation processes, disadvantaging women in STEM. Addressing these biases through training and awareness is critical.

Stereotype Threat:

The fear of confirming negative stereotypes about one's gender can negatively impact performance and confidence. Creating supportive environments that counteract stereotype threat is essential.

The Leaky Pipeline

The "leaky pipeline" refers to the phenomenon where women leave STEM fields at higher rates than men at various stages of their careers.

Retention Strategies:

Implementing retention strategies, such as mentorship, career development programs, and supportive networks, can help to address the leaky pipeline and retain women in STEM careers.

The Future of Women in Science and Technology

Emerging Trends

Emerging trends in science and technology offer new opportunities for women to contribute and lead.

Interdisciplinary Research:

The growing importance of interdisciplinary research, which integrates knowledge from different fields, creates opportunities for women to apply diverse perspectives and expertise.

Tech Entrepreneurship:

The rise of tech entrepreneurship provides avenues for women to innovate and lead in technology. Supporting women entrepreneurs through funding, mentorship, and networks is crucial.

Global Perspectives

Promoting gender equality in STEM on a global scale requires addressing unique challenges faced by women in different regions.

Access to Education:

Ensuring access to quality STEM education for girls and women worldwide is fundamental. Initiatives that provide scholarships, build schools, and support female students in underserved areas are vital.

Cultural Norms:

Addressing cultural norms and societal expectations that discourage women from pursuing STEM careers is essential for achieving global gender equality in science and technology.

Conclusion

Women have made invaluable contributions to science and technology throughout history and continue to break new ground in these fields. While significant progress has been made in promoting gender equality in STEM, ongoing efforts are needed to address persistent challenges and barriers.

Encouraging more women to pursue and persist in STEM careers requires a multifaceted approach, including educational initiatives, mentorship, supportive workplace policies, and global efforts to ensure access and equity. By fostering an inclusive and supportive environment, we can unlock the full potential of women in science and technology, driving innovation and progress for all.

The achievements of pioneering women like Marie Curie, Ada Lovelace, and contemporary leaders such as Frances Arnold and Jennifer Doudna, serve as powerful reminders of the impact women can have in STEM. As we look to the future, continued advocacy and action are essential for creating a world where women and men can equally contribute to and benefit from advancements in science and technology.

Chapter 13
Economic Empowerment and Microfinance

Introduction

Economic empowerment is crucial for the overall advancement of women's rights and gender equality. It involves providing women with the resources, opportunities, and autonomy to improve their economic status. Microfinance, a financial service that offers small loans to individuals who lack access to traditional banking services, has emerged as a powerful tool in this regard. This chapter explores the importance of economic empowerment for women, the role of microfinance in fostering this empowerment, and the broader impact of these initiatives on communities and economies globally.

The Importance of Economic Empowerment

Enhancing Women's Autonomy

Economic empowerment allows women to make decisions about their own lives and futures. With financial resources and opportunities, women can:

Invest in Education:

Financial independence enables women to pursue higher education and professional training, enhancing their skills and job prospects.

Healthcare Access:

Empowered women can afford better healthcare for themselves and their families, leading to improved health outcomes.

Decision-Making Power:

Economic independence increases women's influence in household and community decisions, promoting gender equality at various levels of society.

Reducing Poverty

Empowering women economically has a significant impact on poverty reduction. Studies have shown that women are more likely than men to invest their earnings in their families and communities, leading to:

Improved Child Welfare:

Increased income in the hands of women often results in better nutrition, education, and healthcare for children.

Community Development:

Women's economic participation fosters community growth, as they are more likely to support local businesses and social initiatives.

Promoting Economic Growth

Women's participation in the economy boosts overall economic growth. When women have equal access to economic opportunities, the following benefits arise:

Increased Productivity:

Diverse workforces are more innovative and productive, driving business and economic growth.

Expanded Markets:

Women as entrepreneurs and consumers expand markets and create new economic opportunities.

Enhanced Development:

Gender equality in economic participation contributes to broader social and economic development goals.

The Role of Microfinance

Origins and Evolution

Microfinance emerged as a response to the financial exclusion of the poor, particularly women, from traditional banking systems. The concept gained prominence with the work of Dr. Muhammad Yunus and the Grameen Bank in Bangladesh in the 1970s.

Grameen Bank Model:

This model provides small loans to groups of women, who collectively guarantee each other's loans. The approach has demonstrated high repayment rates and significant social impact.

Expansion and Innovation:

Microfinance has evolved to include various services, such as savings accounts, insurance, and financial literacy training, expanding its reach and effectiveness.

Empowering Women through Microfinance

Microfinance has proven particularly effective in empowering women for several reasons:

Access to Capital:

Microfinance provides women with the capital needed to start and grow businesses, which they are often unable to obtain from traditional banks.

Entrepreneurship and Employment:

Loans enable women to become entrepreneurs, creating jobs for themselves and others in their communities.

Financial Inclusion:

By offering financial services to underserved populations, microfinance promotes broader financial inclusion and stability.

Case Studies and Success Stories

Bangladesh: The Grameen Bank

The Grameen Bank, founded by Dr. Muhammad Yunus, has been a pioneer in using microfinance to empower women.

High Repayment Rates:

The bank's innovative group lending model has resulted in repayment rates exceeding 95%.

Poverty Reduction:

Grameen Bank's loans have helped lift millions of women out of poverty by enabling them to start small businesses and increase their incomes.

Social Impact:

Beyond economic benefits, the bank's programs have improved literacy rates, healthcare access, and overall quality of life for its borrowers and their families.

India: Self-Employed Women's Association (SEWA)

SEWA is a trade union of women workers in the informal sector in India, which has utilized microfinance to support its members.

Integrated Services:

SEWA offers a range of financial services, including loans, savings, and insurance, along with vocational training and support.

Empowerment and Advocacy:

By combining financial services with advocacy and support, SEWA has empowered women to fight for their rights and improve their economic conditions.

Community Development:

SEWA's holistic approach has led to significant community development, including improved infrastructure and social services.

Kenya: Kenya Women Finance Trust (KWFT)

KWFT is one of Kenya's largest microfinance institutions, focusing on empowering women through financial services.

Tailored Products:

KWFT offers products tailored to the needs of women, including loans for small businesses, agriculture, and education.

Impact on Lives:

KWFT's services have enabled women to start businesses, increase their incomes, and improve their families' living standards.

Gender Equality:

KWFT's success has contributed to greater gender equality and economic participation of women in Kenya.

Challenges and Criticisms of Microfinance

Sustainability and Scalability

While microfinance has achieved notable successes, it faces challenges related to sustainability and scalability.

Financial Viability:

Ensuring that microfinance institutions (MFIs) remain financially viable while serving the poorest populations is a significant challenge.

Scalability:

Scaling microfinance programs to reach more women, especially in remote and underserved areas, requires substantial resources and infrastructure.

Impact Measurement

Assessing the true impact of microfinance on women's economic empowerment and broader development goals can be complex.

Metrics and Evaluation:

Developing accurate metrics and evaluation methods to measure the long-term impact of microfinance initiatives is essential for understanding their effectiveness.

Holistic Impact:

Microfinance should be evaluated not only on financial outcomes but also on social and psychological impacts, such as increased confidence and autonomy.

Over-Indebtedness

The risk of over-indebtedness is a critical issue in microfinance.

Responsible Lending:

Ensuring responsible lending practices and providing financial literacy training can help mitigate the risk of borrowers becoming over-indebted.

Regulation and Oversight:

Effective regulation and oversight of MFIs are necessary to protect borrowers and ensure ethical practices.

Broader Impact of Economic Empowerment Initiatives

Community and Societal Benefits

Economic empowerment of women through initiatives like microfinance has broader benefits for communities and societies.

Community Development:

Empowered women often invest in their communities, leading to improved infrastructure, education, and social services.

Gender Equality:

Economic empowerment initiatives contribute to gender equality by challenging traditional gender roles and promoting women's participation in economic and social life.

Economic Growth:

Increased economic participation of women drives overall economic growth and development.

Policy and Advocacy

Supporting economic empowerment and microfinance initiatives requires strong policy frameworks and advocacy efforts.

Government Support:

Governments can play a crucial role by creating supportive policies, providing funding, and facilitating partnerships with NGOs and private sector organizations.

Advocacy and Awareness:

Advocacy efforts are essential to raise awareness about the importance of women's economic empowerment and to mobilize support from various stakeholders.

Conclusion

Economic empowerment is a fundamental aspect of advancing women's rights and achieving gender equality. Microfinance has emerged as a powerful tool in this effort, providing women with the resources and opportunities to improve their economic status and contribute to their communities.

While challenges remain, the successes of microfinance initiatives in countries like Bangladesh, India, and Kenya demonstrate the potential for these programs to make a significant impact. By continuing to support and expand economic empowerment initiatives, we can unlock the full potential of women and drive progress towards a more equitable and prosperous world for all.

As we move forward, it is crucial to address the challenges of sustainability, impact measurement, and over-indebtedness, while also fostering supportive policies and advocacy efforts. Through collective action and commitment, we can create a future where women everywhere have the economic power to shape their own destinies and contribute to the well-being of their families, communities, and societies.

Chapter 14
Global Perspectives on Women's Rights

Introduction

The status of women's rights varies widely across different regions of the world. While significant progress has been made in many areas, numerous challenges remain. This chapter examines the current state of women's rights globally, highlighting both advancements and ongoing struggles. It explores the cultural, social, and political factors that influence women's rights in various countries, providing a comprehensive overview of the diverse experiences of women worldwide.

Africa

Progress

Legal Reforms:

Many African countries have implemented legal reforms to enhance women's rights. For instance, Rwanda has achieved gender parity in its parliament, with women holding 61% of the seats.

Education:

There has been a substantial increase in girls' enrollment in primary and secondary education across the continent. Countries like Kenya and Uganda have made strides in promoting girls' education through initiatives such as free primary education and targeted scholarships.

Economic Participation:

Women are increasingly participating in the labor force and entrepreneurial activities. Microfinance institutions, such as Kenya Women Finance Trust (KWFT), have empowered women to start and expand businesses.

Challenges

Gender-Based Violence:

Despite legal reforms, gender-based violence remains a pervasive issue. In South Africa, high rates of domestic violence and sexual assault persist.

Cultural Practices:

Harmful cultural practices such as female genital mutilation (FGM) and child marriage continue to affect millions of girls and women, particularly in countries like Somalia and Mali.

Political Participation:

While some countries have made progress, women's political participation remains limited in many parts of Africa due to entrenched patriarchal norms and inadequate implementation of gender quotas.

Asia

Progress

Education and Health:

Significant strides have been made in improving women's access to education and healthcare. In countries like Japan and South Korea, women's literacy rates and life expectancy are high.

Economic Opportunities:

Women in countries like China and India are increasingly entering the workforce and contributing to economic growth. Initiatives such as the Self-Employed Women's Association (SEWA) in India support women in the informal sector.

Legal Rights:

Legal frameworks in several Asian countries have been strengthened to protect women's rights. For example, India has enacted laws against domestic violence and sexual harassment in the workplace.

Challenges

Gender Discrimination:

Persistent gender discrimination limits women's opportunities in many parts of Asia. In India and Pakistan, women often face barriers to employment and are underrepresented in leadership roles.

Human Trafficking:

Human trafficking remains a critical issue, particularly in Southeast Asia. Women and girls are often trafficked for forced labor and sexual exploitation.

Political Representation:

Women's political representation is low in many Asian countries. In Japan, women hold only about 10% of parliamentary seats, reflecting significant gender disparities in political leadership.

Middle East

Progress

Education:

Access to education for women and girls has improved in several Middle Eastern countries. In Iran, more than half of university students are women.

Health:

Maternal health has seen improvements, with better access to prenatal and postnatal care in countries like Saudi Arabia and Jordan.

Economic Participation:

Efforts to increase women's participation in the workforce are underway. Saudi Arabia has introduced reforms to allow women to work in various sectors and drive cars.

Challenges

Legal Restrictions:

Women in many Middle Eastern countries face legal restrictions that limit their rights. In Saudi Arabia, despite recent reforms, women still require male guardians' permission for various activities.

Cultural Norms:

Deep-rooted cultural and religious norms often restrict women's freedoms and opportunities. In Afghanistan, the resurgence of the Taliban has severely curtailed women's rights and access to education.

Violence and Conflict:

Women in conflict zones, such as Syria and Yemen, face heightened risks of violence, displacement, and limited access to basic services.

Europe

Progress

Gender Equality Policies:

European countries are leaders in promoting gender equality through comprehensive policies and legislation. The Nordic countries, in particular, have high levels of gender equality in education, employment, and politics.

Economic Empowerment:

Women's economic participation is strong, with countries like Germany and France implementing policies to support work-life balance, such as parental leave and childcare services.

Political Representation:

European countries have high rates of women's political representation. In Sweden, women make up nearly half of the parliament, reflecting successful gender quotas and inclusive policies.

Challenges

Pay Gap:

Despite progress, the gender pay gap persists across Europe. Women generally earn less than men for equivalent work, with significant disparities in countries like the United Kingdom and Germany.

Violence Against Women:

Domestic violence and sexual harassment remain serious issues. Countries like Spain have implemented robust measures to combat gender-based violence, but challenges persist.

Migration and Integration:

Female migrants and refugees face additional barriers to integration, including language barriers, discrimination, and limited access to employment opportunities.

Latin America

Progress

Political Leadership:

Latin America has seen notable female political leaders, such as Michelle Bachelet in Chile and Dilma Rousseff in Brazil, reflecting growing political representation of women.

Legal Reforms:

Many countries have strengthened legal protections for women. Argentina and Mexico have enacted comprehensive laws to combat gender-based violence and support survivors.

Social Movements:

Vibrant social movements, such as the #NiUnaMenos movement against femicide in Argentina, have raised awareness and driven policy changes to protect women's rights.

Challenges

Violence Against Women:

High rates of femicide and domestic violence are major issues. In countries like Honduras and El Salvador, women face extreme levels of violence and limited access to justice.

Economic Inequality:

Women in Latin America often face economic inequality, with higher rates of informal employment and lower wages compared to men.

Reproductive Rights:

Access to reproductive health services, including abortion, is restricted in many countries. In Brazil and Argentina, recent debates and legislative changes reflect ongoing struggles over reproductive rights.

North America

Progress

Legal Protections:

The United States and Canada have strong legal frameworks to protect women's rights. Laws such as the Violence Against Women Act (VAWA) in the U.S. and the Canadian Human Rights Act provide critical protections.

Economic Participation:

Women in North America have high levels of workforce participation and are increasingly represented in leadership roles. Companies are adopting policies to promote gender diversity and inclusion.

Political Representation:

Women are gaining ground in politics, with record numbers of women elected to the U.S. Congress and Canadian Parliament in recent years.

Challenges

Pay Inequality:

Despite progress, the gender pay gap remains a significant issue. Women in the U.S. earn about 82 cents for every dollar earned by men, with even larger disparities for women of color.

Work-Life Balance:

Balancing work and family responsibilities remains a challenge. The lack of affordable childcare and paid parental leave policies in the U.S. affects women's economic opportunities.

Violence and Discrimination:

Gender-based violence and discrimination persist. The #MeToo movement has highlighted widespread issues of sexual harassment and assault, leading to increased advocacy and policy changes.

Oceania

Progress

Political Leadership:

Women have achieved significant political leadership in countries like New Zealand, where Jacinda Ardern serves as Prime Minister, exemplifying strong female leadership.

Gender Equality Policies:

Australia and New Zealand have comprehensive gender equality policies, promoting women's rights in various sectors, including employment, education, and health.

Education and Health:

Women in Oceania generally have high levels of access to education and healthcare, contributing to improved quality of life and economic participation.

Challenges

Violence Against Women:

Domestic violence is a significant issue in Oceania. In Australia, one in six women has experienced physical or sexual violence from a current or former partner.

Economic Inequality:

Women in Oceania face economic inequality, with lower wages and higher rates of part-time work compared to men.

Indigenous Women:

Indigenous women in Australia and New Zealand face additional challenges, including higher rates of violence, discrimination, and limited access to services.

Conclusion

The status of women's rights varies widely across the globe, shaped by cultural, social, and political factors unique to each region. While significant progress has been made in many areas, ongoing challenges remain that require continued advocacy and action.

Understanding the diverse experiences of women worldwide is crucial for developing effective strategies to promote gender equality. By addressing the specific needs and challenges faced by women in different regions, we can work towards a more equitable and just world for all.

As we move forward, it is essential to celebrate the achievements of women and to recognize the importance of continued efforts to protect and advance women's rights globally. Through collective action and sustained commitment, we can create a future where women everywhere have the opportunity to thrive and contribute to their societies.

Chapter 15
Women and Environmental Activism

Introduction

Women have been at the forefront of environmental activism for decades, playing crucial roles in advocating for sustainability and climate change mitigation. This chapter explores the significant contributions of women to environmental movements, highlighting key figures and initiatives that have driven progress in this field. By examining the unique perspectives and approaches women bring to environmental activism, we can better understand the vital link between gender equality and environmental sustainability.

Historical Context and Emergence of Women in Environmental Activism

Early Pioneers

Women have long been involved in environmental protection, with some of the earliest activists emerging in the 19th and early 20th centuries.

Rachel Carson:

Often considered the mother of the modern environmental movement, Carson's 1962 book *Silent Spring* exposed the dangers of pesticides and sparked widespread environmental awareness and regulatory changes.

Wangari Maathai:

A Kenyan environmentalist and political activist, Maathai founded the Green Belt Movement in 1977, which focuses on tree planting, environmental conservation, and women's rights. She was awarded the Nobel Peace Prize in 2004 for her contributions to sustainable development, democracy, and peace.

Key Movements and Contributions

The Green Belt Movement

Founded by Wangari Maathai, the Green Belt Movement is one of the most influential environmental organizations led by women.

Tree Planting and Conservation:

The movement has planted over 51 million trees in Kenya, combating deforestation, restoring ecosystems, and improving livelihoods.

Empowerment of Women:

By involving women in tree planting and environmental conservation, the movement has empowered thousands of women economically and socially, fostering community development and resilience.

Chipko Movement

In the 1970s, the Chipko Movement emerged in India as a grassroots environmental campaign to protect forests.

Tree-Hugging Protests:

Led by rural women, the movement used nonviolent resistance, with women physically embracing trees to prevent logging. This tactic gained global attention and successfully halted deforestation in several areas.

Community Involvement:

The movement highlighted the crucial role of women in forest conservation and the sustainable use of natural resources, emphasizing their deep connection to their environment.

Climate Action and Advocacy

Women have been at the forefront of global climate action, advocating for stronger policies and practices to combat climate change.

Greta Thunberg:

The Swedish teenager's "Fridays for Future" movement has inspired millions of young people worldwide to demand urgent action on climate change. Thunberg's activism has brought global attention to the climate crisis, influencing policy discussions and public opinion.

Christiana Figueres:

As the Executive Secretary of the UN Framework Convention on Climate Change (UNFCCC), Figueres played a pivotal role in negotiating the Paris Agreement in 2015, a landmark international accord aimed at limiting global warming.

Women's Unique Contributions to Environmental Sustainability

Integrating Gender Perspectives

Women often bring unique perspectives to environmental issues, integrating gender considerations into sustainability efforts.

Community Engagement:

Women are typically more involved in household and community-level activities, making them essential players in implementing sustainable practices and raising environmental awareness.

Holistic Approaches:

Women's approaches to environmental activism often emphasize holistic and community-based solutions, addressing interconnected social, economic, and environmental challenges.

Sustainable Agriculture and Food Security

Women play a critical role in sustainable agriculture and food security, particularly in rural areas.

Agroecology:

Women farmers frequently adopt agroecological practices, such as crop diversification, organic farming, and water conservation, which contribute to sustainable land management and resilience to climate change.

Food Sovereignty:

Women's involvement in local food systems and traditional knowledge helps promote food sovereignty, ensuring that communities have control over their food production and consumption.

Challenges and Barriers

Gender Inequality

Despite their significant contributions, women environmental activists often face gender-based challenges and barriers.

Discrimination and Exclusion:

Women are frequently marginalized in environmental decision-making processes, limiting their influence on policies and initiatives.

Violence and Harassment:

Female environmental activists are at risk of violence, harassment, and intimidation, particularly in regions with weak governance and human rights protections.

Access to Resources

Limited access to resources and support hinders women's ability to engage in environmental activism effectively.

Funding and Training:

Women-led environmental organizations often struggle to secure funding and training opportunities, constraining their capacity to implement impactful projects.

Property Rights:

In many regions, women lack secure land and property rights, restricting their ability to manage and conserve natural resources sustainably.

Global Initiatives and Support for Women Environmental Activists

International Recognition

International organizations and initiatives are increasingly recognizing and supporting the role of women in environmental activism.

UN Women:

The United Nations entity for gender equality and the empowerment of women supports various programs and initiatives to enhance women's leadership in environmental sustainability.

Global Environment Facility (GEF):

The GEF integrates gender considerations into its projects, ensuring that women's contributions to environmental sustainability are recognized and supported.

Grassroots Movements

Grassroots movements led by women continue to drive significant environmental change at the local and global levels.

Indigenous Women's Movements:

Indigenous women are leading efforts to protect their lands and biodiversity, advocating for their rights and traditional knowledge in environmental governance.

Youth-Led Activism:

Young women activists are at the forefront of the climate movement, using innovative strategies and digital platforms to mobilize communities and influence policy.

Case Studies

Vandana Shiva: Navdanya Movement

Vandana Shiva, an Indian environmentalist and food sovereignty advocate, founded the Navdanya movement to promote biodiversity conservation and organic farming.

Seed Sovereignty:

Navdanya focuses on preserving indigenous seeds and promoting seed sovereignty, ensuring that farmers have control over their seeds and agricultural practices.

Women Farmers:

The movement empowers women farmers by providing training and resources, enabling them to adopt sustainable farming practices and improve their livelihoods.

Berta Cáceres: Lenca Indigenous Rights and Environmental Protection

Berta Cáceres, a Honduran environmental and indigenous rights activist, co-founded the Council of Popular and Indigenous Organizations of Honduras (COPINH).

River Protection:

Cáceres led efforts to protect the Gualcarque River from the construction of the Agua Zarca Dam, advocating for the rights of the Lenca people and the preservation of their environment.

Legacy of Activism:

Despite her assassination in 2016, Cáceres' legacy continues to inspire environmental and indigenous rights movements globally, highlighting the risks faced by female activists.

Conclusion

Women have made invaluable contributions to environmental activism, advocating for sustainable practices and climate change mitigation worldwide. Their unique perspectives and approaches have led to significant advancements in environmental protection and community resilience.

However, women environmental activists still face numerous challenges, including gender inequality, limited access to resources, and violence. It is crucial to support and amplify the voices of women in environmental movements, recognizing their vital role in achieving sustainable development and climate justice.

By fostering inclusive and equitable approaches to environmental activism, we can harness the full potential of women to drive positive change and build a more sustainable and just world for future generations.

Chapter 16
Legal Milestones in Women's Rights

Introduction

The advancement of women's rights has been significantly shaped by various legal milestones across the globe. Landmark cases, treaties, and conventions have played crucial roles in promoting gender equality and protecting women's rights. This chapter explores these significant legal milestones, detailing their impact on the global women's rights movement and highlighting key instruments like the Convention on the Elimination of All Forms of Discrimination Against Women (CEDAW).

Early Legal Milestones

The Married Women's Property Acts

United Kingdom (1870 and 1882):

These Acts allowed married women to own and control property in their own right, marking a significant step towards gender equality in property rights.

United States:

Similar laws were enacted across various states, starting with Mississippi in 1839, allowing women to own property, enter contracts, and engage in business independently of their husbands.

Suffrage Movements and Voting Rights

New Zealand (1893):

The first self-governing country to grant women the right to vote, setting a precedent for other nations.

United States (1920):

The 19th Amendment to the U.S. Constitution granted women the right to vote after decades of activism by suffragists.

United Kingdom (1918 and 1928):

Women over 30 gained the right to vote in 1918, and equal voting rights were established in 1928, allowing all women over 21 to vote.

Post-World War II Legal Milestones

Universal Declaration of Human Rights (1948)

Article 2:

Affirms that everyone is entitled to all the rights and freedoms set forth in the Declaration, without distinction of any kind, including sex.

Article 21:

Recognizes the right to participate in government and the equal access to public service, laying the groundwork for women's political rights globally.

Convention on the Elimination of All Forms of Discrimination Against Women (CEDAW) (1979)

Overview:

Often described as an international bill of rights for women, CEDAW was adopted by the United Nations General Assembly in 1979 and has been ratified by 189 states.

Key Provisions:

CEDAW addresses various forms of discrimination against women, including in areas such as political and public life, education, employment, health, and family relations.

Impact:

The Convention has led to the adoption of numerous national laws and policies aimed at eliminating gender discrimination and promoting equality.

Landmark Legal Cases

United States

Roe v. Wade (1973):

The U.S. Supreme Court decision that recognized a woman's constitutional right to choose to have an abortion, significantly impacting reproductive rights.

Ledbetter v. Goodyear Tire & Rubber Co. (2007):

Although the initial ruling was against Lilly Ledbetter, it led to the Lilly Ledbetter Fair Pay Act of 2009, which strengthened protections against pay discrimination.

India

Vishaka v. State of Rajasthan (1997):

This landmark judgment led to the establishment of guidelines to prevent sexual harassment at the workplace, which were later codified into law as the Sexual Harassment of Women at Workplace (Prevention, Prohibition and Redressal) Act in 2013.

Triple Talaq Case (2017):

The Supreme Court of India declared the practice of instant triple talaq (divorce) among Muslims unconstitutional, protecting Muslim women's rights within marriage.

European Union

Equal Pay Directive (1975):

Established the principle of equal pay for equal work, a foundational legal standard for gender equality in the workplace across EU member states.

Case C-184/83 Hofmann v. Barmer Ersatzkasse (1984):

The European Court of Justice ruled on the importance of maternity leave, influencing policies to support working mothers.

Regional Treaties and Conventions

Inter-American Convention on the Prevention, Punishment, and Eradication of Violence Against Women (Belém do Pará) (1994)

Overview:

This treaty was adopted by the Organization of American States (OAS) and aims to prevent, punish, and eradicate violence against women in the Americas.

Key Provisions:

It recognizes the right of women to be free from violence and establishes mechanisms for the protection and defense of women's rights.

African Charter on Human and Peoples' Rights (Maputo Protocol) (2003)

Overview:

The Protocol to the African Charter on Human and Peoples' Rights on the Rights of Women in Africa, commonly known as the Maputo Protocol, addresses women's rights comprehensively.

Key Provisions:

It covers various issues, including harmful practices, reproductive rights, economic empowerment, and political participation, providing a robust framework for the promotion of women's rights in Africa.

Recent Legal Milestones

Istanbul Convention (2011)

Overview:

The Council of Europe Convention on preventing and combating violence against women and domestic violence, known as the Istanbul Convention, sets comprehensive standards for protecting women from violence.

Key Provisions:

It emphasizes prevention, protection, prosecution, and integrated policies to combat all forms of violence against women.

Domestic Workers Convention (C189) (2011)

Overview:

Adopted by the International Labour Organization (ILO), this convention aims to protect the rights of domestic workers, a workforce predominantly made up of women.

Key Provisions:

It ensures fair terms of employment, decent working conditions, and protection from abuse and harassment for domestic workers globally.

Impact of Legal Milestones

Advancement of Gender Equality

Policy Reforms:

These legal milestones have spurred policy reforms worldwide, leading to the adoption of gender equality measures in various sectors.

Awareness and Advocacy:

Legal frameworks have raised awareness about women's rights and provided a basis for advocacy and activism, empowering women to demand their rights.

Challenges and Ongoing Efforts

Implementation Gaps:

Despite significant legal advancements, challenges remain in the implementation and enforcement of women's rights laws.

Cultural and Societal Barriers:

Deep-rooted cultural and societal norms continue to hinder the full realization of women's rights in many regions.

Conclusion

The journey towards achieving women's rights has been marked by numerous significant legal milestones. From early property rights reforms to contemporary international treaties, these legal instruments have played a crucial role in advancing gender equality and protecting women's rights globally.

While substantial progress has been made, ongoing efforts are required to address implementation challenges and overcome cultural and societal barriers. By continuing to strengthen legal frameworks and ensuring their effective enforcement, we can move closer to a world where women's rights are fully realized and gender equality is achieved.

Chapter 17
The Role of NGOs and Grassroots Movements

Introduction

Non-governmental organizations (NGOs) and grassroots movements have been pivotal in advancing women's rights across the globe. These entities operate at various levels, from local communities to international platforms, advocating for policy changes, raising awareness, and providing essential services. This chapter explores the significant impact of NGOs and grassroots movements, highlighting successful campaigns and the strategies employed to effect change.

The Emergence and Evolution of NGOs and Grassroots Movements

Historical Context

Early 20th Century:

The women's suffrage movement, one of the earliest forms of organized grassroots activism, saw the formation of groups such as the National American Woman Suffrage Association (NAWSA) in the United States and the Women's Social and Political Union (WSPU) in the United Kingdom.

Post-World War II:

The establishment of the United Nations and its various agencies provided a platform for international advocacy on women's rights, leading to the creation of numerous NGOs dedicated to gender equality.

Growth and Global Influence

1970s-1980s:

The second-wave feminist movement spurred the formation of NGOs and grassroots organizations focused on a wide range of issues, including reproductive rights, workplace equality, and violence against women.

1990s-Present:

The proliferation of digital communication has enabled these organizations to connect globally, coordinate campaigns, and mobilize support more effectively.

Key NGOs in Women's Rights Advocacy

International NGOs

Amnesty International

Focus:

Human rights advocacy, including women's rights.

Campaigns:

Initiatives such as "My Body My Rights," which addresses issues like sexual and reproductive health and rights.

Human Rights Watch

Focus:

Investigating and reporting on human rights abuses worldwide.

Campaigns:

Reports and advocacy efforts on topics such as gender-based violence and discriminatory laws.

Oxfam International

Focus:

Poverty alleviation and social justice, with a significant emphasis on women's rights.

Campaigns:

Programs that empower women economically and address issues like unpaid care work.

National and Regional NGOs

Equality Now

Focus:

Legal advocacy for women's rights.

Campaigns:

Efforts to end practices such as female genital mutilation (FGM) and child marriage.

Women for Women International

Focus:

Supporting women survivors of war.

Campaigns:

Programs providing vocational training, education, and psychosocial support to empower women in post-conflict regions.

Grassroots Movements and Their Impact

Notable Grassroots Movements

#MeToo Movement

Origin:

Initiated by activist Tarana Burke in 2006 and gained global prominence in 2017.

Impact:

Highlighted the prevalence of sexual harassment and assault, leading to significant cultural shifts and policy changes in various sectors.

Ni Una Menos (Not One Less)

Origin:

Started in Argentina in 2015 in response to increasing femicide rates.

Impact:

Expanded across Latin America, raising awareness about gender-based violence and influencing legislative reforms.

Self-Employed Women's Association (SEWA)

Origin:

Founded in India in 1972 by Ela Bhatt.

Impact:

Empowered millions of informal women workers through unionization, access to credit, healthcare, and education.

Strategies for Effecting Change

Advocacy and Lobbying

Policy Advocacy:

NGOs and grassroots movements often engage in policy advocacy, lobbying for legislative changes and the implementation of international treaties such as CEDAW.

Strategic Litigation:

Organizations like Equality Now use strategic litigation to challenge discriminatory laws and practices in courts around the world.

Awareness Campaigns and Education

Public Awareness Campaigns:

Initiatives like the UN Women's "HeForShe" campaign aim to engage men and boys in the fight for gender equality.

Educational Programs:

NGOs often run educational programs to raise awareness about women's rights and provide training on issues such as reproductive health and financial literacy.

Community Empowerment

Grassroots Organizing:

Empowering local communities to advocate for their rights through training, capacity building, and leadership development.

Economic Empowerment:

Providing resources and support for women to start businesses, gain employment, and achieve economic independence.

Use of Technology and Social Media

Digital Advocacy:

Utilizing social media platforms to mobilize support, spread awareness, and coordinate campaigns globally.

Online Platforms:

Creating online platforms for resource sharing, networking, and advocacy, such as the Association for Women's Rights in Development (AWID).

Successful Campaigns and Their Outcomes

The Campaign to End FGM

Overview:

NGOs like Equality Now and grassroots organizations in Africa have led successful campaigns to end female genital mutilation.

Outcomes:

Significant legal reforms in countries such as Kenya and Egypt, increased awareness, and community-based efforts to change cultural practices.

The Global Campaign for Equal Pay

Overview:

Initiatives by organizations like the International Labour Organization (ILO) and UN Women to address the gender pay gap.

Outcomes:

Legislative changes in several countries, corporate commitments to pay transparency, and increased public awareness.

Reproductive Rights Advocacy

Overview:

NGOs such as Planned Parenthood and grassroots movements have campaigned for reproductive rights, including access to contraception and safe abortion.

Outcomes:

Legalization of abortion in countries like Ireland and Argentina, expanded access to reproductive healthcare services, and broader public support for reproductive rights.

Challenges and Future Directions

Funding and Resources

Sustainability:

Many NGOs and grassroots movements face challenges in securing consistent funding, which affects their sustainability and impact.

Resource Allocation:

Ensuring that resources reach grassroots organizations, especially those in marginalized and underserved communities.

Political and Cultural Barriers

Resistance:

Advocacy efforts often encounter resistance from conservative political and cultural forces.

Backlash:

Activists can face backlash, including threats and violence, particularly in regions with weak legal protections for women's rights.

Expanding Reach and Inclusivity

Intersectionality:

Emphasizing the importance of intersectional approaches that address the diverse experiences of women based on race, class, sexuality, and other factors.

Global Solidarity:

Strengthening global networks and alliances to support local movements and amplify their impact.

Conclusion

NGOs and grassroots movements have been instrumental in advancing women's rights globally, achieving significant legal and social changes through advocacy, awareness campaigns, community empowerment, and the strategic use of technology. Despite facing numerous challenges, these organizations continue to drive progress toward gender equality, demonstrating the power of collective action and sustained advocacy.

By building on successful strategies and fostering inclusive, intersectional approaches, NGOs and grassroots movements can further their impact and contribute to a world where women's rights are universally respected and upheld.

Chapter 18
The Future of Women's Rights

Introduction

As the global landscape continues to evolve, the future trajectory of the women's rights movement is poised to address both emerging issues and enduring challenges. This chapter speculates on the potential advancements and ongoing struggles for gender equality in a rapidly changing world. It explores technological innovations, shifting socio-political dynamics, and the continuing fight for equality, aiming to provide a comprehensive outlook on the future of women's rights.

Emerging Issues

Technological Advancements and Digital Rights

Digital Gender Divide:

While technology offers new avenues for empowerment, it also risks exacerbating existing inequalities. Women and girls in many parts of the world still have less access to digital technologies and the internet.

Online Harassment and Safety:

As more aspects of life move online, addressing cyberbullying, online harassment, and digital violence against women becomes crucial. Initiatives to ensure safe online spaces for women and girls will be imperative.

AI and Automation:

The rise of artificial intelligence (AI) and automation could disproportionately affect women, particularly in sectors where they are overrepresented. Ensuring gender-sensitive policies in the tech industry and equitable access to STEM education will be critical.

Climate Change and Environmental Justice

Climate Vulnerability:

Women, especially in developing countries, are more vulnerable to the impacts of climate change due to their roles in agriculture, water collection, and household management. Policies must address these vulnerabilities and involve women in climate action and decision-making.

Ecofeminism:

The intersection of environmental and gender justice, or ecofeminism, is likely to gain more traction, advocating for sustainable practices that also promote gender equality.

Economic Inequality and Labor Rights

Gig Economy:

The gig economy and informal work sectors, where many women are employed, lack protections and benefits. Advocating for labor rights and protections in these sectors will be essential.

Pay Equity:

Despite progress, the gender pay gap persists. Future efforts will need to focus on transparency in pay practices, enforcement of equal pay laws, and challenging occupational segregation.

Potential Advancements

Legal and Policy Reforms

Comprehensive Legislation:

More countries are expected to adopt comprehensive gender equality laws, encompassing areas like domestic violence, reproductive rights, and workplace discrimination.

Global Standards:

Strengthening international standards and ensuring countries adhere to conventions like CEDAW will remain a priority. Efforts to integrate gender perspectives into all UN treaties and global agreements will also be crucial.

Education and Empowerment

Access to Education:

Continued efforts to ensure that girls and women have equal access to quality education will be fundamental. This includes addressing barriers such as early marriage, poverty, and gender-based violence in schools.

Leadership Development:

Programs aimed at developing women's leadership skills in politics, business, and community organizations will help create a new generation of female leaders.

Health and Reproductive Rights

Universal Healthcare:

Advocacy for universal healthcare systems that include comprehensive reproductive health services will be essential. This includes access to contraception, safe abortion services, and maternal healthcare.

Mental Health:

Addressing the mental health needs of women, including those related to gender-based violence and discrimination, will become increasingly important.

Ongoing Struggles for Equality

Socio-Cultural Barriers

Patriarchy and Traditional Norms:

Patriarchal systems and traditional gender norms continue to impede progress. Grassroots efforts to challenge these norms and promote gender-equitable attitudes will be vital.

Intersectionality:

Recognizing and addressing the multiple, intersecting forms of discrimination faced by women based on race, class, sexuality, disability, and other factors will remain a significant challenge.

Political Participation and Representation

Gender Quotas:

Implementing and enforcing gender quotas in political representation can ensure that women have a voice in governance. Efforts will also focus on creating inclusive political environments that support women's full participation.

Global Movements:

Continued support for global feminist movements and solidarity across borders will help amplify women's voices and push for systemic changes.

Technological Innovations

Blockchain and Financial Inclusion

Cryptocurrencies and Blockchain:

These technologies have the potential to enhance financial inclusion for women, particularly in developing countries where access to traditional banking is limited.

Microfinance and Digital Banking:

Expanding microfinance initiatives through digital platforms can empower women economically and support entrepreneurship.

Health Technology

Telemedicine:

Increasing access to healthcare through telemedicine, particularly in rural and underserved areas, can improve women's health outcomes.

Reproductive Health Apps:

The development of apps and digital tools to provide information and support for reproductive health will be crucial.

Global Solidarity and Collaboration

International Partnerships

Global Alliances:

Building and strengthening international alliances and networks will help coordinate efforts and share best practices for advancing women's rights.

South-South Cooperation:

Promoting collaboration among developing countries can foster mutual support and innovation in addressing gender equality issues.

Funding and Resources

Sustainable Funding:

Ensuring sustainable funding for women's rights organizations, especially grassroots groups, will be necessary for continued progress.

Corporate Responsibility:

Encouraging private sector involvement through corporate social responsibility (CSR) initiatives that support gender equality can provide additional resources and influence.

Conclusion

The future of women's rights is shaped by both emerging challenges and potential advancements. As the world rapidly changes, the women's rights movement must adapt and innovate, leveraging new technologies, advocating for comprehensive legal reforms, and addressing the intersectional nature of discrimination.

The ongoing struggle for gender equality will require sustained efforts from individuals, organizations, governments, and international bodies. By fostering global solidarity, ensuring inclusive approaches, and promoting innovative solutions, we can continue to advance women's rights and work towards a future where gender equality is a reality for all.

Chapter 19
Personal Stories of Empowerment

Introduction

Personal stories of empowerment provide a deeply human perspective on the global impact of women's rights. These narratives showcase the resilience, strength, and determination of women from diverse backgrounds who have overcome significant challenges and made remarkable contributions to their communities. By sharing these stories, we celebrate the progress made and inspire future generations to continue the fight for gender equality.

The Story of Malala Yousafzai: A Champion for Education

Background

Early Life:

Born in Mingora, Pakistan, Malala Yousafzai grew up in a region where the Taliban often attacked girls' schools.

Advocacy:

From a young age, Malala became an outspoken advocate for girls' education, blogging under a pseudonym for the BBC about life under Taliban rule and her desire for education.

Overcoming Challenges

Assassination Attempt:

In 2012, Malala was shot in the head by a Taliban gunman while on a school bus. She survived and was flown to the United Kingdom for treatment.

Recovery and Advocacy:

Following her recovery, Malala continued her advocacy on a global scale, founding the Malala Fund to champion education for girls worldwide.

Impact

Nobel Peace Prize:

In 2014, Malala became the youngest-ever recipient of the Nobel Peace Prize.

Global Influence:

Her story has inspired millions and has significantly raised awareness about the importance of education for girls.

The Story of Wangari Maathai: Environmental and Social Activism

Background

Early Life:

Born in rural Kenya, Wangari Maathai was the first woman in East and Central Africa to earn a doctorate degree.

Green Belt Movement:

In 1977, she founded the Green Belt Movement, which focused on environmental conservation, tree planting, and women's rights.

Overcoming Challenges

Government Opposition:

Wangari faced significant opposition from the Kenyan government, including arrests and physical assaults.

Persistence:

Despite the challenges, she persisted in her environmental and social activism, mobilizing thousands of women to plant trees and advocate for their rights.

Impact

Nobel Peace Prize:

In 2004, Wangari Maathai became the first African woman to receive the Nobel Peace Prize.

Legacy:

Her work has led to the planting of over 50 million trees and has empowered many women in Kenya and beyond to engage in environmental activism.

The Story of Nadia Murad: Advocate Against Human Trafficking

Background

Early Life:

Nadia Murad was born in Kocho, a Yazidi village in northern Iraq. In 2014, ISIS militants attacked her village, killing many and taking women and girls captive.

Captivity and Escape:

Nadia was held captive and subjected to sexual violence before she managed to escape.

Overcoming Challenges

Public Advocacy:

Despite the trauma she endured, Nadia chose to speak out about her experiences to raise awareness about the plight of the Yazidi people and the horrors of human trafficking.

Global Platform:

She has addressed the United Nations and met with various world leaders to advocate for the rights of trafficking survivors.

Impact

Nobel Peace Prize:

In 2018, Nadia Murad was awarded the Nobel Peace Prize, alongside Dr. Denis Mukwege, for their efforts to end the use of sexual violence as a weapon of war.

Initiatives:

She founded Nadia's Initiative, an organization dedicated to rebuilding communities in crisis and advocating for survivors of sexual violence.

The Story of Rigoberta Menchú Tum:
Indigenous Rights Activism

Background

Early Life:

Born in Guatemala to a poor indigenous family, Rigoberta Menchú Tum witnessed and experienced the oppression and violence faced by indigenous communities.

Activism:

She became an activist, fighting for the rights of indigenous people and against the atrocities committed during the Guatemalan Civil War.

Overcoming Challenges

Exile:

Due to her activism, Rigoberta faced threats to her life and was forced into exile in Mexico.

Continued Advocacy:

From exile, she continued her advocacy, drawing international attention to the plight of indigenous peoples in Guatemala.

Impact

Nobel Peace Prize:

In 1992, she was awarded the Nobel Peace Prize for her work in promoting indigenous rights and social justice.

Legacy:

Rigoberta Menchú Tum has become a global symbol of indigenous resistance and empowerment.

The Story of Tarana Burke: Founder of the #MeToo Movement

Background

Early Life:

Tarana Burke grew up in the Bronx, New York, and began her career in activism at a young age, focusing on issues of racial and gender inequality.

#MeToo Movement:

In 2006, she founded the Me Too movement to support survivors of sexual violence, particularly women of color.

Overcoming Challenges

Amplification:

The movement gained widespread attention in 2017 when actress Alyssa Milano used the hashtag #MeToo, which quickly went viral.

Ongoing Efforts:

Tarana has continued to lead and expand the movement, focusing on systemic change and support for survivors.

Impact

Cultural Shift:

The #MeToo movement has led to a significant cultural shift, raising awareness about the prevalence of sexual harassment and assault and holding perpetrators accountable.

Global Movement:

It has inspired similar movements worldwide, empowering survivors to speak out and demand justice.

The Story of Leymah Gbowee: Peace and Reconciliation

Background

Early Life:

Leymah Gbowee grew up in Liberia and experienced the brutal civil war that ravaged her country.

Women of Liberia Mass Action for Peace: In 2003, she led a nonviolent movement of women from different religious and ethnic backgrounds to demand peace in Liberia.

Overcoming Challenges

Nonviolent Protest:

Leymah and her fellow activists faced threats and violence but remained steadfast in their commitment to nonviolence.

Peace Agreement:

Their efforts culminated in the Accra Peace Accord, which ended the Second Liberian Civil War.

Impact

Nobel Peace Prize:

In 2011, Leymah Gbowee was awarded the Nobel Peace Prize alongside Ellen Johnson Sirleaf and Tawakkol Karman for their nonviolent struggle for the safety of women and for women's rights to full participation in peace-building work.

Legacy:

Leymah continues to advocate for peace, women's rights, and social justice through various initiatives and organizations.

Conclusion

These personal stories of empowerment illustrate the profound impact that individual women can have on their communities and the world. Through their courage, resilience, and determination, these women have not only overcome significant challenges but have also inspired millions and driven meaningful change.

As we look to the future of women's rights, these narratives remind us of the power of personal stories in advancing the movement. They highlight the importance of continued advocacy, solidarity, and support for women and girls worldwide, ensuring that their voices are heard and their rights are upheld.

Chapter 20
A Call to Action

Introduction

The journey through the history and ongoing struggles for women's rights has been both enlightening and inspiring. As we conclude this exploration, it is essential to recognize that the fight for gender equality is far from over. Each of us has a role to play in advancing women's rights and creating a more just and equitable world. This chapter provides a comprehensive call to action, offering practical steps individuals can take to support gender equality.

Educate Yourself and Others

Learn About Gender Issues

Read and Research:

Stay informed about gender issues by reading books, articles, and reports on women's rights. Understanding the historical context and current challenges is crucial for effective advocacy.

Attend Workshops and Seminars:

Participate in workshops, seminars, and webinars focused on gender equality and women's rights to deepen your knowledge and stay updated on recent developments.

Raise Awareness

Share Information:

Use your social media platforms to share articles, videos, and resources on women's rights issues. Amplifying credible information helps educate others and spread awareness.

Host Discussions:

Organize discussion groups or book clubs to talk about gender equality. Engaging in conversations with friends, family, and colleagues can foster a deeper understanding and encourage collective action.

Support Women's Organizations

Donate

Financial Contributions:

Support NGOs and grassroots organizations that advocate for women's rights by making financial donations. Even small contributions can make a significant difference.

In-Kind Donations:

Offer in-kind donations such as clothing, hygiene products, or professional services to organizations that provide direct support to women in need.

Volunteer

Offer Your Time:

Volunteer with local or international organizations working to advance women's rights. Whether it's mentoring young girls, helping at a shelter, or providing professional skills, your time can have a meaningful impact.

Pro Bono Services:

If you have professional skills such as legal expertise, counseling, or marketing, consider offering your services pro bono to women's rights organizations.

Advocate for Policy Changes

Engage with Policymakers

Contact Representatives:

Write letters, send emails, or call your local, state, and national representatives to advocate for policies that promote gender equality. Share your views on issues such as equal pay, reproductive rights, and violence against women.

Participate in Public Consultations:

Attend public consultations and town hall meetings to voice your support for gender-equal policies and legislation.

Support Legislation

Campaign for Change:

Join or support campaigns advocating for specific legislative changes. Participating in organized efforts can amplify your voice and increase the chances of success.

Vote:

Exercise your right to vote and support candidates who prioritize gender equality and women's rights. Encourage others to do the same.

Foster Equality in the Workplace

Promote Inclusive Practices

Advocate for Policies:

Push for policies that promote gender equality in your workplace, such as paid parental leave, flexible working hours, and anti-harassment measures.

Mentorship Programs:

Support or initiate mentorship programs that help women advance in their careers. Providing guidance and opportunities for growth can help break the glass ceiling.

Address Bias

Unconscious Bias Training:

Advocate for and participate in unconscious bias training sessions to help identify and mitigate biases in the workplace.

Equal Opportunities:

Ensure that hiring, promotions, and pay practices are transparent and equitable. Challenge and address any disparities you observe.

Support Women in Leadership

Encourage Participation

Mentor Women Leaders:

Mentor and support women who aspire to leadership roles in various fields, including politics, business, and community organizations.

Nominate Women:

Actively nominate and support women for leadership positions, awards, and recognitions. Highlighting their achievements can inspire others and promote gender diversity in leadership.

Amplify Voices

Provide Platforms:

Offer platforms for women to share their stories, ideas, and expertise. Whether through conferences, panels, or publications, amplifying women's voices is crucial.

Advocate for Representation:

Push for gender diversity in decision-making bodies and boards. Representation matters, and having women in leadership roles can drive systemic change.

Challenge Social Norms

Address Stereotypes

Challenge Gender Norms:

Actively challenge and question traditional gender norms and stereotypes in everyday life. Promote and practice behaviors that support gender equality.

Educate the Young:

Teach children about gender equality from an early age. Encourage them to pursue their interests and challenge gender roles.

Support Survivors of Violence

Believe and Support:

Believe and support survivors of gender-based violence. Provide emotional and practical support, and help them access resources and justice.

Promote Safe Spaces:

Advocate for and support the creation of safe spaces for women in schools, workplaces, and communities.

Join Global Movements

Participate in Campaigns

Global Campaigns:

Join global campaigns such as #HeForShe, #MeToo, and International Women's Day activities. Participating in these movements helps raise awareness and mobilize action on a larger scale.

Solidarity Actions:

Participate in solidarity actions such as marches, protests, and online campaigns to show support for women's rights globally.

Conclusion

The fight for women's rights is a collective endeavor that requires the active participation of individuals from all walks of life. By educating ourselves and others, supporting women's organizations, advocating for policy changes, fostering equality in the workplace, supporting women in leadership, challenging social norms, and joining global movements, we can each contribute to advancing gender equality.

This call to action is not just about supporting women; it is about creating a more just and equitable world for all. Every step taken towards gender equality benefits society as a whole, promoting justice, economic growth, and social cohesion. Let us commit to being part of the change, supporting one another, and continuing the fight for a future where gender equality is a reality for everyone.

Epilogue

Reflecting on Progress and Paving the Way Forward

Reflecting on Progress

As we conclude this comprehensive exploration of women's rights, it is essential to reflect on the remarkable progress made over the past centuries. The journey towards gender equality has been long and arduous, filled with significant milestones and inspirational stories of resilience, courage, and determination.

Historical Milestones

Early Advocacy:

The foundational work of early feminists like Mary Wollstonecraft, Elizabeth Cady Stanton, and Sojourner Truth laid the groundwork for the women's rights movement. Their writings and activism highlighted the injustices faced by women and called for equal rights and opportunities.

Suffrage Movement:

The global fight for women's suffrage marked a pivotal moment in the history of women's rights. Securing the right to vote empowered women politically and set the stage for further advancements in gender equality.

Second-Wave Feminism:

The rise of feminism in the 20th century, including the second-wave movement, brought attention to a broader range of issues such as reproductive rights, workplace discrimination, and sexual harassment. Landmark publications like "The Feminine Mystique" and the formation of organizations like NOW (National Organization for Women) were instrumental in these efforts.

Legislative Achievements

Equal Pay Act:

Enacted in various countries, the Equal Pay Act aimed to address gender pay disparities and ensure that women receive equal pay for equal work.

Reproductive Rights:

Legal milestones such as Roe v. Wade in the United States and the establishment of reproductive health services worldwide have significantly advanced women's reproductive rights.

CEDAW:

The Convention on the Elimination of All Forms of Discrimination Against Women (CEDAW) has been a critical international treaty advocating for women's rights and gender equality globally.

Social and Cultural Shifts

Women in Leadership:

The increasing presence of women in leadership roles across politics, business, science, and technology signifies a profound cultural shift towards gender equality. Figures like Angela Merkel, Jacinda Ardern, and Malala Yousafzai have become symbols of women's potential to lead and inspire.

Media Representation:

Progress in the portrayal of women in media has also been notable. More diverse and accurate representations of women have challenged stereotypes and influenced societal attitudes towards gender roles.

The Importance of Continued Advocacy and Solidarity

While significant progress has been made, the journey towards gender equality is far from complete. Continued advocacy and solidarity are essential to address the persistent and emerging challenges that women face globally.

Persistent Challenges

Gender-Based Violence:

Violence against women, including domestic violence, sexual assault, and human trafficking, remains a critical issue. Continued efforts to combat these forms of violence and support survivors are crucial.

Economic Inequality:

The gender pay gap, occupational segregation, and lack of access to economic resources still hinder women's economic empowerment. Policies and initiatives that promote economic equality are needed.

Political Participation:

Despite progress, women are still underrepresented in political decision-making bodies. Efforts to ensure gender parity in politics and support women's political participation must continue.

Emerging Issues

Technological Inequality:

As technology becomes increasingly central to all aspects of life, ensuring that women have equal access to digital tools and opportunities is vital. Addressing online harassment and creating safe digital spaces for women are also important.

Climate Change:

Women, particularly in developing countries, are disproportionately affected by climate change. Integrating gender perspectives into climate policies and involving women in environmental decision-making is essential for sustainable solutions.

Collective Responsibility

Achieving gender equality is not the responsibility of a few; it requires the collective efforts of individuals, communities, organizations, and governments. Each of us has a role to play in advancing women's rights and ensuring that future generations inherit a world where gender equality is a reality.

Individual Actions

Education and Awareness:

Stay informed about gender issues and share knowledge with others. Engage in conversations about gender equality and challenge stereotypes and biases.

Support and Advocacy:

Support women's rights organizations through donations, volunteering, and advocacy. Advocate for policies that promote gender equality in your community and workplace.

Organizational Efforts

Inclusive Practices:

Implement and promote inclusive practices in workplaces, schools, and communities. Ensure that policies and programs are designed to support gender equality.

Support for Women's Leadership:

Provide opportunities and support for women to take on leadership roles. Mentor and sponsor women in their professional and personal growth.

Governmental and Global Initiatives

Policy and Legislation:

Governments must enact and enforce laws that protect women's rights and promote gender equality. International cooperation and adherence to global standards like CEDAW are essential.

Global Solidarity:

Foster global solidarity through international partnerships and support for women's rights movements worldwide. Collaborative efforts can amplify impact and drive systemic change.

Conclusion

Reflecting on the progress made in the journey towards women's rights, we celebrate the achievements and acknowledge the challenges that remain. The stories of women who have overcome obstacles and made significant contributions to their communities inspire us to continue the fight for gender equality.

As we look to the future, it is imperative that we remain committed to advocating for women's rights and fostering a culture of equality and inclusion. By working together, we can create a world where gender equality is not just a goal but a reality for all. Let us embrace our collective responsibility and take action to pave the way forward for future generations, ensuring that the legacy of the women's rights movement endures and flourishes.

THE END!